CW00348849

Misfits & Hybrids

Architectural Artifacts for the 21st-Century City

Misfits & Hybrids

Architectural Artifacts for the 21st-Century City

Ferda Kolatan

Routledge
Taylor & Francis Group

NEW YORK AND LONDON

Designed cover: Ferda Kolatan. Image credit: Caleb Ehly & Joonsung Lee

First published 2024
by Routledge
605 Third Avenue, New York, NY 10158

and by Routledge
4 Park Square, Milton Park, Abingdon, Oxon, OX14 4RN

Routledge is an imprint of the Taylor & Francis Group, an informa business

© 2024 Ferda Kolatan

The right of Ferda Kolatan to be identified as author of this work has been asserted in accordance with sections 77 and 78 of the Copyright, Designs and Patents Act 1988.

All rights reserved. No part of this book may be reprinted or reproduced or utilised in any form or by any electronic, mechanical, or other means, now known or hereafter invented, including photocopying and recording, or in any information storage or retrieval system, without permission in writing from the publishers.

Trademark notice: Product or corporate names may be trademarks or registered trademarks, and are used only for identification and explanation without intent to infringe.

Library of Congress Cataloging-in-Publication Data
A catalog record for this title has been requested

ISBN: 9781032396101 (hbk)
ISBN: 9781032396118 (pbk)
ISBN: 9781003350569 (ebk)

DOI: 10.4324/9781003350569

Typeset in Bagatela, Archivo, Times New Roman
by Ferda Kolatan

Publisher's Note: This book has been prepared from camera-ready copy provided by the author.

Printed and bound in Great Britain by
TJ Books Limited, Padstow, Cornwall

To my father, Metin Kolatan

the first person who made me want to draw

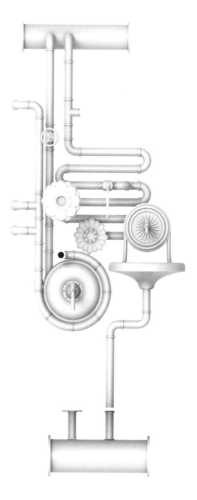

Fig. 1.1 Grace Kim & Rachel Lee, Hybrid Artifact, rendering,
Cairo Studio, University of Pennsylvania Weitzman School of Design, 2016.

Preface   ix

Misfits & Hybrids
Architectural Artifacts for the 21st-Century City   1

   Urban Misfits   8
   Hybrid Artifacts   20
   From Parts to Objects   24
   Another Kind of Architectural Fantasy   30

Istanbul
Unscripted Immediacies of Past, Present, and Future   39

   Unlikely Affinities   44
   Ambiguous Architecture   70
   Withdrawn Landmark   82
   Machinic Garden   110

Cairo
Real Fictions   139

   Informal Assets   144
      Informal Assets Catalogue   146
      The Ring Road   166
      The Gabkhana   174
   Over/Under   180

New York
Authenticity without Origin   205

   Estranged Monument I   208
   Estranged Monument II   226

Acknowledgments   260

Index   262

Preface

My interest in architectural misfits and hybrids has developed over the course of many years, stemming from a fascination with things that possess an air of oddity, eclecticism, and contextual incongruity. At the outset, this interest was driven by a curiosity toward the idiosyncratic–an attraction to objects, buildings, and urban conditions that deviated from perceived norms and added a playful component to the city.

Over time, this curiosity spawned deeper inquiries concerning the latent potential of misfits and hybrids for architectural design. Given the ubiquitous and varied manner in which they populate urban environments, I wondered what an architecture that incorporated and learned from these odd material accretions might look like. What opportunities would arise for innovative design and practical implementation? How would this architecture express diverse subjects such as history, culture, politics, aesthetics, and the environment?

Questions like these have become the focal point of my academic research. Between 2016 and 2021, my teaching assistants and I led six cohorts of students from the University of Pennsylvania Weitzman School of Design to Cairo, Istanbul, and New York. Within these complexly layered urban landscapes, we experimented with design tactics derived from mismatched elements and developed a wide range of projects in different scales and circumstances.

The resulting hybrid artifacts are presented here in a whimsical and provocative style, aiming to convey the spontaneous allure of encountering misfit conditions while strolling through the city. The architecture conjured by these artifacts reveals a treasure trove of surprising qualities often hiding in plain sight, easily overlooked in the bustle of urban life. Ultimately, the work serves as a heartfelt ode to those aberrations and anomalies born of the cosmopolitan postindustrial city.

Misfits & Hybrids

Architectural Artifacts for the 21st-Century City

> Everything changes, nothing perishes.
>
> – OVID, *Metamorphoses*

The encounter of architectural oddities in the city is familiar to most of us. They come in all shapes and sizes, appearing before us without much notice or fanfare. A quirky entanglement of mundane mechanical pipes and delicate architectural ornamentation, for instance, or a historical edifice awkwardly nestled in harsh and uncaring contemporary surroundings. An elevated highway cutting mercilessly through a residential block, or some remnants of decaying buildings merging with other architectural components into new aggregate forms. More often than not, we tend to ignore such anomalies, dismissing them as random occurrences, hardly noticing their existence at all. And yet, once in a while, these peculiar arrangements do capture our attention. Appearing at times fleeting and humorous and at others lasting and contemplative, their ambiguous nature affects our experience of the city and instills in us a sense of curiosity and wonder.

Given the ubiquity of these conditions and their potential to engage us positively with our built environment, a series of questions arises: Why is it that these oddities are rarely, if ever, appreciated as architecture? After all, are they not the outcomes of the very same processes–albeit at different stages in their development and life cycle–that also yield the buildings and urban spaces we valorize as architectural accomplishments? Weren't they once designed, fabricated, and utilized within the same types of material and cultural practices that undergird all urban architecture? Why is it then that we, as experts or laypeople, cling to such an inflexible categorical mindset when determining what constitutes architecture in the first place? Moreover, what untapped design opportunities do we forfeit by delineating so strictly between architecture and non-architecture?

As change sweeps over buildings in its typically haphazard, uncontrolled, and unforeseeable fashion, architecture becomes riddled with aberrations. Despite the general consensus within the architectural community on the privileging of change, difference, and plurality as the preeminent tenets of our era, we aren't accustomed to appreciating the value of buildings that have outlasted their original purpose and transitioned into a state of indeterminable flux. Time thus poses a distinct challenge to design, namely, that of how to deal proactively with the physical consequences it invariably exerts on objects. However, given the ubiquity and inevitability of these transformations–aging, alterations, changing contexts, and juxtapositions with other objects–their effects should be considered as essential components of these forms rather than defects. Viewed in this light, these "blemishes" or irregularities have the potential to generate new and unexpected principles for design.

This reconception requires a new framework. For, the appearance of something as idiosyncratic may, to a large extent, simply indicate the absence of a proper disciplinary context within which such conditions can be adequately explored, debated, and evaluated. This framework would need to facilitate the revaluation of perceived aberrations and the design strategies according to which they can be recast as valid and desirable forms of architecture. The concept of the city, historically malleable and evolving, would need to expand further to embrace all of its physical components regardless of their functional or aesthetic conditions. The city must be conceived as a vast depository of objects, ceaselessly changing and recombining into new formations that embody the dynamic collision of diverse forces that constitutes the urban condition. At once concealed and in plain sight, the city of misfits and hybrids emerges cunningly from the background, consisting of renegade assemblies and odd kinships, both intriguing and strange.[1]

* * *

As will be argued over the following chapters, much can be gained from this readjusted framework as architectural oddities are omnipresent, versatile, and express significant characteristics of large postindustrial cities. For instance, they reflect municipal protocols and local material practices, embody cultural customs, and often possess–through their mixed composition–an allure more immediate and relatable than that of more conventional buildings and landmarks. In addition, this framework opens up a largely unexplored territory for design experimentation, where existing buildings and building components may be recombined into unlikely configurations with new functional and programmatic purposes. This falls somewhat under the rubric adaptive reuse, with which it shares commonalities. Both prioritize tactical interventions over large-scale renewal strategies and favor the reappropriation of existing assets over rebuilding.

However, what distinguishes the approach outlined in this book from other reuse-oriented approaches are the specific design and representational techniques employed, along with a primary focus on conditions commonly perceived as unfavorable, irrelevant, or irretrievably devalued within the context of everyday urban life. Through vivid snapshots that evoke the fleeting nature of spontaneous urban encounters, the projects here assemble new possible architectures from the "fallout" that all large metropolitan cities invariably produce.

What binds these projects together, and serves as a foundational argument for the book, is not their affiliation with a particular place, even though the designs do incorporate autochthonous cultural characteristics by utilizing existing building stock. Nor is it the strict adherence to the norms and standards typically associated with specific building scales or types that guide much of organized architectural practice. Instead, the overarching theme is that odd and idiosyncratic architecture represents a global phenomenon, one that intensifies along with a city's complexity and disorderliness. Thus, the depository of objects is inevitably expanding, opening up new territories and challenging common definitions of what constitutes architecture's significance and value in the 21st-century city.

* * *

The reasoning behind the terminology of *misfits* and *hybrids* will be discussed in more detail in the following two chapters, "Urban Misfits" and "Hybrid Artifacts." For now, it suffices to say that *misfits* refers to urban oddities and irregularities produced by the passage of time, while *hybrids* denotes the artifacts produced by extrapolating distinct features from said misfits (**Figs. 1.2, 1.3**). Crucially, both terms invoke a deviation from normative standards of how things ought to look and act and, by extension, reflect a critical understanding of the reality that these standards constitute.

In his essay, "In Search of the Lost Real," philosopher Alan Badiou asks: "Is the real never just found, discovered, encountered, invented, but always invariably the source of a commandment, the figure of an iron law? Is it always necessarily the originator of rules?"[2] Here, Badiou distinguishes between two types of reality: one as the source of "commandments and laws," and the other as a condition that may be "encountered," as if by chance or happenstance, or "invented" through willful acts of imagination. Misfits and hybrids can be understood as expressions of the tension inherent in this distinction. Misfits are found objects to be encountered or

3

discovered, and hybrids are the novel forms and potential realities they inspire. As such, Badiou's notion of the real offers a compelling conceptual guide for situating hybrid artifacts within contemporary discourse. The discrepancies between a reality of orders and one of spontaneous encounter and invention are the pervading concern of this book.

In transposing Badiou's sociopolitical critique of the prevailing real to the realm of architecture, an interesting correlation emerges. Commandments and laws hold paramount authority in architecture as well. This is evident in the multitude of rules and regulations set by building departments, city councils, landmark and preservation commissions, and similar entities, as well as the orders stipulated in canonical texts. However, of greater significance to the argument presented here are the effects these laws have on the general public's perception of architecture as constituting an immutable reality. For something to be recognized as architecture, that entity needs to conform to the category's established criteria. Anything that lies beyond this reality–structures and buildings that cannot be sufficiently categorized according to the prescribed rules and laws that define architecture–finds itself in a peculiar liminal space.

Misfits and hybrids inhabit this liminal space. By evading the strict classifications that delineate real architecture, they raise the question: What exactly are they? Non-architecture? Bad architecture? Do they represent the absence of architecture altogether? Could it be that this state of ambiguity, instead of indicating an inadequacy, is in fact a source from which alternative realities may emerge– architectural realities constituted by diverse acts of discovery and invention? Presumably, this architecture would follow a very different set of principles than those of urban agencies, developers, and the discipline itself. Moreover, this architecture would inevitably take on different physical characteristics and would be more open to being shaped by its public, fostering a more personal and proactive approach toward the city.

Despite this oppositional stance, misfits and hybrids do not advocate the wholesale abolition of rules and regulations to usher in a form of urban anarchy. Nor do they promote a utopian ideal, projected into a faraway or abstract future, unburdened by the constraints of the everyday. Instead, they aim to capture and capitalize on the gaps, tensions, and mismatches that constitute the byproducts of the ordered and regulated mechanisms of the city. Like a dish concocted from leftovers and perishing ingredients, misfits and hybrids may supplement a meticulously prepared "recipe" with improvisational flair by incorporating remnants and surplus elements that might otherwise go overlooked.

* * *

Fig. 1.2 Andrew Homick & Yiren Weng, mixed-media sectional model, Istanbul Studio, University of Pennsylvania Weitzman School of Design, 2018.

This hybrid artifact underscores the odd adjacencies among the organic, tectonic, structural, mechanical, and graphic elements of a residential building in Istanbul. The potential for unforeseen spatial and formal connections between the graffiti-covered retaining wall and the adjacent sidewalk is explored through the exposure of concealed cavities within the building's basement, elevator, and mechanical shafts.

In order to fully leverage the potential of misfits, we must release the hold of the enduring categories that define architecture. The third chapter "From Parts to Objects," outlines how misfits and hybrids introduce a variation to the long disciplinary tradition of hierarchical part-to-whole relationships. By categorizing all building components, regardless of their size or function with respect to the whole structure, as objects, the conception and assembly of hybrid artifacts is based on the equality between parts and wholes. This shift in terminology from *parts* and *wholes* to *objects* signals a departure from the ethics and aesthetics governed by design principles rooted in notions of purity and anthropocentrism.[3] Classical or modern systems of order, founded on established proportions and idealizations, as well as functionalist principles aiming to confine form, function, and program within rigid hierarchies and value systems, are playfully disregarded by hybrids. All available objects can be seized and integrated into opportunistic constellations. The hybrid's odd aesthetic stems from this opportunism and is facilitated by the gradual erosion of established ordering principles amid the intricate workings of the contemporary city.

The fourth chapter, "Another Kind of Architectural Fantasy" addresses questions of architectural representation, positioning the hybrid within the genre of the architectural fantasy drawing, and tracing its lineage to 18th-century predecessors like the *capriccio* and *rocaille*. The notably mixed character of the rocaille, with its rather bizarre amalgamations of real and fictitious elements, stands as a particularly compelling precursor. To consider hybrids as architectural fantasy might initially seem a curious choice, given the projects' embeddedness in actual urban conditions and their emphasis on actionable tactics. Yet, the intertwined exploration of concepts of real and fiction, the broader cultural narrative that misfits and hybrids convey in the absence of directives from clients or competition briefs, and the representational formats they assume, all indicate their affinity with architectural fantasy.

Following these introductory chapters, a wide range of case studies comprise the central parts of this book. Some inquiries take the form of detailed projects, while others are more fleeting evocations. Various sites across Istanbul, Cairo, and New York serve as the testing grounds for these misfit and hybrid tactics, encompassing diverse scales, architectural programs, and urban challenges. Chosen for their substantial size, complex histories, and diverse cosmopolitanism, these cities have produced misfit conditions both jarring and subtle. While each city possesses a distinct character, they all grapple with issues that are endemic to the global postindustrial megacity. Chief among these issues is an escalating trend toward architectural uniformity and rampant unchecked real estate speculation, gentrification, densification, heightened waste production and carbon footprint, pollution, traffic congestion, and so forth. Left in the wake of these challenges, neighborhoods, buildings, and infrastructural components fall into disarray, providing ample opportunities for exploring hybridization techniques.

NOTES

1 Donna Haraway coined the term "oddkin" to describe and advocate for novel forms of human/ nonhuman ecologies and relationships. While Haraway primarily directs her exploration towards peculiar interspecies kinships, this concept has served as our guiding principle in embracing notions of odd material hybridizations. Donna Haraway, *Staying with the Trouble: Making Kin in the Chthulucene* (Durham: Duke University Press, 2016).

2 According to French philosopher Alain Badiou, the notion of the real has become an instrument of power and oppression in today's capitalist societies. Badiou writes, "Today, the word 'real' is mostly used as intimidation," followed by the question, "But is the real never just found, discovered, encountered, invented, but always invariably the source of a commandment, the figure of an iron law?" Alain Badiou, *Auf der Suche nach dem Verlorenen Realen* (Wien: Passagen Verlag, 2016), 11. The English translation is provided by the author.

3 By "purity" and "anthropocentricism," I refer to classicist and humanist ideologies, which, with notable exceptions, have predominantly guided the formation of the architectural canon in the Western tradition.

Fig. 1.3 Caleb Ehly & Joonsung Lee, mixed-media sectional model,
Istanbul Studio, University of Pennsylvania Weitzman School of Design, 2019.

This hybrid artifact is composed by modifying residual shapes, textures, and colors
found within a historic courtyard in Istanbul into a densely layered conglomerate.

Urban Misfits

Contemporary cities are shaped by the unlikely adjacencies, intersections, and overlaps of objects that are vastly different in function, age, origin, and scale. Buildings, building-parts, infrastructural elements, street furniture, and other urban bits and pieces accrue over time into perplexing yet often compelling crossovers and misalignments. Once we pay closer attention, we encounter such incongruous compositions wherever we turn: an old Beaux-Arts facade, on which floral ornamentations involuntarily interweave with haphazard bundles of colorful electrical cables; a modest residential home pushing hard against the massive foundations of a steel bridge; a corroding cast-iron truss sharply cutting through a vestigial brick firewall; a cluster of gleaming plastic satellite dishes hovering over traditional clay roof tiling; an elevated multilane highway stretching menacingly over a heap of loosely arranged wooden market stalls; an ancient oak tree leaning against a traffic light in an awkward gesture of embrace.

Seemingly too random and pointless to be considered serious subjects for theoretical or design inquiry, misfits, despite their ubiquity, fade into the background of daily urban hustle, destined to be overlooked. They are, however, anything but trivial. By embodying idiosyncrasies, tensions, and contradictions, misfits reflect many of the unsung qualities of urban life itself. In this revelatory sense, they may be understood not as useless remnants but rather as the potential constituents of an altogether different kind of city. This city is governed not by the coordinated efforts of planners, developers, and architects but by the dynamic processes put in motion by time and happenstance, forged into matter by the countless interactions they spawn.

In this city of misfits, the conventional framing of architecture as a carefully planned, controlled, and orderly endeavor is subverted. Instead, chance encounters, unlikely entanglements, and unplanned acts of collaboration take precedence. Previously intact or coherent functions, programs, stylistic features, and design protocols are out-of-sync, obsolete, or intertwined with other elements, resulting in odd configurations. The traces of these jumbled histories add to the misfit's characteristic tension, and arguably, its appeal. Acts of reintegration can lead to more sustainable design ecologies, and they bring to the fore the suppressed, forgotten, and fragmentary storylines inscribed within misfits.[4]

Unperturbed by preordained determinations, misfits refract an intriguing kaleidoscopic picture of the underbelly of contemporary cities, calling attention to urban

Figs. 1.4, 1.5, 1.6 Urban Misfits, Istanbul, 2019. (Photograph courtesy Andrew Homick.)

Three examples of misfit conditions found in cities. Misfits are unanticipated yet often intriguing adjacencies, overlaps, and intersections existing among urban components, characterized by distinctive details, such as the water pipe peeking out from beneath the firehose cabinet (Fig. 1.4), the uneasy convergence of three walls (Fig. 1.5), or the "hovering" gate (Fig. 1.6). Perceived as manifestations of urban tensions outside a hierarchically determined framework of component relations, misfit components have a semiautonomous quality that distinguishes them from mere building parts.

processes that often go unnoticed. This city within a city cannot be sufficiently captured within existing urban theories and models as it lacks clear associations with intentional concepts, whether derived from lofty ideals spanning from the Greek polis to the modern functionalist metropolis, or organic definitions of urban growth arising from programmatic patterns, geography, or topography. Furthermore, misfits cannot be merely evaluated as byproducts of late-capitalist urban transformations.[5] While these transformations often lead to the proliferation of misfits, they do not offer a meaningful understanding of misfits' architectural potential. Misfits are predominantly seen as symptoms of dysfunction or as the material evidence of the failure of monolithic planning strategies undermined by the volatile and incalculable dynamic of the city.

In order to establish a quasi-theoretical framework to address the potential of misfits, the city is envisioned as a *depository of objects,* disregarding the hierarchical relationships and material values that are commonly attached to them.[6] In the depository, all physical entities regardless of scale, type, or complexity are treated as equals, and together they comprise a diverse repertoire from which new and unexpected constellations can be forged. *Objects* encompasses everything we perceive in a unified state, but these entities are not necessarily discrete. For instance, a sidewalk, a house, a roof, a window, a doorknob, or a satellite dish would all be considered as individual objects even though a house might also contain some of these other elements. Anything we conceive of as a *thing* is regarded as an object.

This radical flattening of the city is a necessary first step for identifying misfits and transforming them into a new combinatorial or hybrid architecture.

This flattening approach toward the material conditions of the city does not ignore the intricate underlying historical forces that shape it. Rather, as we will see in each of the projects that follow, these histories are understood as irrevocably baked into urban objects and therefore always already in the mix. Each object is an expression of the various material, technological, cultural, social, and economic circumstances that produced it. However, in the depository, these objects take on a semiautonomous quality that allows for unforeseen possibilities. Take, for example, a security booth in Istanbul: a small, enclosed structure featuring stone details, partial brick walls, a domed roof, a single window, electrical boxes, conduits, and a camera (**Fig. 1.7**). Our immediate perception of this constellation might lead to a series of deductions and qualifications: a once precious building made of stone was restored with generic brick fillings, haphazardly retrofitted with electrical equipment, and a technical device was installed for surveillance purposes. All these relational assessments, while perhaps factual, undermine these objects' potential to engage a different context or foster relationships beyond what might immediately occur to their beholder as the reasons for their existence.

In contrast, once viewed as equal, semiautonomous objects, the components of the security booth become focal points in and of themselves, calling attention to their own material properties such as shape, color, and texture. Observed in this flattened mode, the booth's facade appears less like a random patchwork of successive repairs and retrofits and more like a meaningful composition of discontinuities and abrupt adjacencies. The symmetry of the electrical boxes, their off-center position, the window with its gray metal cover situated diagonally from the similarly shaped electrical boxes, the intertwining of gray stone blocks with red brick, and even the surveillance camera's physical affinity to the dome's spire comprise a dynamic architectural mosaic, oscillating between tensions and unexpected kinships. Embracing these tensions and kinships while loosening the strands of established relationships in which components are confined to predetermined roles sets the stage for hybrid design.

Misfits and Environment

In these perilous and unprecedented times of man-made environmental disasters, it is urgent that we explore a wide range of design ideas, strategies, and tactics that deal with existing built structures in more versatile and innovative ways. The reappropriation of existing structures can significantly mitigate the effects of architecture's large carbon footprint and address problems associated with diminishing natural resources and increasing waste production, pollution, and greenhouse gas emissions. While the efforts to cut emissions and protect natural resources–e.g., the use of sustainable building materials or more efficient

Fig. 1.7 Security booth, Istanbul, 2022. (Photograph courtesy Ferda Kolatan.)

renewable energy technologies–are important measures, they predominantly target the operational carbon associated with powering buildings, while ignoring the problem of embodied carbon emissions in buildings and building components.[7] Hybrid architecture, with its focus on the reappropriation of existing structures, confronts this issue head-on.

The most effective way to curb the detrimental consequences of embodied carbon in architecture is to break, as much as possible, the perpetual cycles of building, demolition, and rebuilding that fuel the development, construction, and architecture industries and exacerbate environmental problems. To combat this trend, architecture must shift its focus more progressively toward the revitalization of existing urban structures rather than continue to valorize "new" buildings as its default objective. Whenever possible, architects should work with structures the embodied carbon of which has already been deposited into the world. The demolition and disposal of existing structures only further accelerates carbon emissions.[8] Existing practices of restoration and adaptive reuse address this issue but deal primarily with whole buildings, or significant portions of them, that are considered historically significant or valuable in some way. Our misfit approach seeks to expand the territory of reuse to include fragmentary, disparate, and ordinary elements that are not usually considered valuable. By conceiving of the city as a depository of objects, rather than an accumulation of buildings and infrastructure, the arena for reuse becomes significantly wider. This widening is incredibly significant given that the vast majority of "non-architectural" built matter is not considered for reuse at the end of its presumed life cycle but discarded or simply left to wither.

While the decisions as to which buildings to fix and rehabilitate and which to not are driven foremost by institutional and economic factors, architectural design exploration, like hybrid artifacts, can play an important role. The willingness to deal with structures typically deemed as ugly, impractical, unfeasible, and unrealistic to restore may hinge on our ability to represent them in new scenarios in which they appear both actionable as well as desirable. The case for misfits as a credible addition to the category of structures considered for reuse depends, therefore, on the production of novel imagery that draws our interest and invokes a certain degree of plausibility. To compete with the dominant practices of our day and their perpetual cycles of building and demolition, the potential of reappropriating architectural misfits for reducing carbon emissions associated with new buildings, offsite fabrication, and transportation needs to be complemented with a unique aesthetic that captures its sustainable qualities through intriguing forms.

Misfits and Culture

Many of the properties of misfits that yield potential environmental benefits also provide a unique vantage point through which to understand the diverse cultural circumstances of a place. While we readily attribute cultural significance to edifices like mosques, churches, museums, or palaces, we are much less likely to extend the same courtesy to structures that seem generic to us. In cases where we do recognize the impact of generic architecture on culture, it is usually as a programmatic stage for cultural activities to take place. Street art, for example, including dance, music, and graffiti, routinely incorporates everyday architecture. However, in these instances, cultural value is not perceived as embodied in the material properties and design of individual buildings or architectural components but rather in their ability to blend into the background.

And yet, ordinary buildings or disjointed components are in themselves not devoid of culture. Despite their mundane or fragmentary nature, these structures and components do, in fact, embody the complex, albeit less apparent, histories and customs of a place in their own peculiar ways. Every building element, whether it is a fading ornament, forlorn artisanal detail, or a generic component picked from stock, expresses the stylistic preferences, material choices, and crafting techniques that reveal a community's labor practices and social habits. These objects represent culture just as much as more coherent, well-planned, or fully intact buildings do. In fact, one could argue that misfits reveal a sort of architectural subculture, which stands in vivid contrast to the standardized building practices that dominate the city.

Fig. 1.8 Kethüda Yusuf Efendi Çeşmesi, Istanbul, 2022. (Photograph courtesy Ferda Kolatan.)

There are two distinct benefits to this subordinated status of misfits. Firstly, they bring the fragmentary and multifaceted histories of a place, no matter how insignificant they may seem, to light. For example, the odd juxtaposition between an 18th-century stone fountain enclosure, a recently installed marble fountain emulating a past style, and the drab stucco facades of two 1960s apartment buildings form a curiously captivating ensemble, telling an ongoing tale of shifting customs, preferences, and practices (**Fig. 1.8**). Secondly, the incongruous patchwork of old and new, ordinary and special elements that characterize misfit architecture more closely mirrors the diverse social and cultural habits and experiences of the city's inhabitants. Extracting misfit conditions from a diffuse background grants them individuality, encouraging people to seek them out, interact with, and potentially modify them in the future. These connections between people and buildings are crucial for fostering a sense of belonging, often absent in new developments, and for encouraging spontaneous forms of utilization (and participation), alongside the normative programmatic uses we commonly associate with buildings.[9]

But the cultural value of misfits and hybrids goes beyond their inherent capacity to represent difference and engender new interactions with ordinary and fragmented buildings. As misfits are predominantly residual, paradoxical, and accidental, they offer a record of the miscalculations, oversights, and failures of municipal planning policies and private real estate speculation. This criticality is embedded within misfits as hard evidence of adverse effects of urban machinations. An especially intriguing example of this is the elevated highway in Ezbet Khayrallah, featured in the Cairo section of this book. The severing of a formerly close-knit neighborhood into two parts by a multilane highway has produced an abundance of misfit conditions, which have been appropriated by the residents in spontaneous and unscripted ways (**Fig. 1.9**). This dual capacity of misfits to conjure novel scenarios and embody the failure of planning policies provides an invaluable cultural and sociopolitical lens through which to understand contemporary cities more fully.

Misfits and Aesthetics

How we judge the value of things is inexorably linked to their sensory qualities: how they materialize, what they look and feel like. We navigate the world through these aesthetic discernments, and the world imparts its reality to us through physical matter. Changes, be they societal, cultural, or environmental, affect us materially and are inextricably bound to what we perceive as aesthetic phenomena. Agency itself is cloaked in physical forms through which it becomes legible and proliferates. In the words of Jane Bennett, things have a "calling-power," which speaks to their vitality and autonomy but also their ability to draw us toward them, almost magically, as if an invisible, unquantifiable bond between us existed.[10]

Bennett's notion of calling-power is particularly relevant to this study as it encompasses things that are usually deemed undesirable and useless. For Bennett, this is evidenced by the curious phenomenon of hoarding.[11] The underlying motivation that compels hoarders to collect specific objects is difficult to determine, often described as an urge outside the realm of rational thought. This urge is an aesthetic response to the objects that compose our physical environment; however, according to Bennett, it is also an expression of empathy–a mechanism through which humans show care for the world through mutual companionship, rather than through ownership. To consider the city as a depository of objects, where all things, regardless of their perceived value, can be potentially revitalized in new collaborative acts, is rooted in this very sentiment.

The example of hoarding points to an aesthetic condition in which architectural objects are not validated as "useful" or "beautiful" based on established criteria such as historical or stylistic authenticity, vernacular compatibility, novelty in form, or technological expressiveness.[12] Instead, from within the depository, objects beckon to us precisely because their qualities cannot be neatly captured in a categorical framework. Misfits are too elusive and ambiguous to be confined easily within such boundaries, as they traverse, mend, and undermine. Perhaps such indeterminacy is compelling because it necessitates a moment of reflection and provides refuge from an overly determined world that often feels overbearing and inflexible. Maybe what *calls* the hoarder to a particular, seemingly useless object is precisely this renegade status, its independence from an excessively confining context, and its freedom to be interpreted and imagined in ways beyond its original intent.

The ambiguous aesthetic of misfits arises from their disjointed transitions, abrupt adjacencies, and unexpected overlaps. Often whimsical and peculiar, discomforting and perplexing, they have the power to startle us and disrupt the rhythm of our daily urban experience, appearing at once familiar and strange. The creative potential of estrangement has been extensively discussed by literary critic Viktor Shklovsky in his seminal essay, "Art as Technique." While exploring the concept of "defamiliarization," Shklovsky makes a critical distinction between *knowing* and *perceiving* objects. Knowing (or recognizing) inevitably leads to a diminished aesthetic experience, as Shklovsky states, "after we see an object several times, we begin to recognize it and the object is in front of us and we know about it, but we do not see see it."[13] He proceeds to link the experience of art to an object's innate

Fig. 1.9 Highway Wall, Ezbet Khayrallah, Cairo, 2016. (Photograph courtesy Rachel Lee.)

A miles-long concrete wall bordering the elevated highway is used by local artisans and vendors to showcase plaster artifacts. The challenge posed by the highway barrier, which cuts through a tightly knit community, is transformed into a useful tool for showcasing the material practices and labor customs of the locals. The ad hoc arrangement of decorative plaster rosettes on the wall's coarse concrete surface creates an "accidental" composition and aesthetic. (See also pages 168–71.)

capacity to be perceived autonomously beyond its descriptive properties, to be *seen* before being *known*. In this context, the ambiguity of misfits can be understood as a prolongation of seeing, which becomes *an aesthetic end in itself*.[14] According to Shklovsky, this prolongation of seeing, or perception, can be achieved by making forms "difficult" through deliberate acts of defamiliarization.[15]

Misfits' fragmented, ambiguous, and compound forms, even without the deliberate intervention of artistic technique, already appear defamiliarized and difficult. Misfits openly challenge hierarchical classifications by indiscriminately incorporating urban elements that are perceived as both extraordinary and ordinary, without any preferential distinctions. As exemplified by the projects in this book, even historically renowned buildings produce the same kind of captivating incongruities that mundane ones do (**Fig. 1.10**). The question that preoccupies us, therefore, is not about elevating a so-called "lower" form of architecture to a "higher" status, but rather about how to represent and acknowledge these tensions and misalignments as the source of legitimate architectural expressions. This question provides the foundation for the transformation of misfits into hybrid architecture and draws intriguing parallels to another, more contemporary, discourse on aesthetics centered around the concept of *artification*.

Artification is concerned with the societal processes through which entities are elevated to the status of art. It explores the mechanisms according to which we attribute special value to certain objects, considering them to transcend the realm of the everyday and attain significance on an altogether different plane. Examples of this phenomenon include Duchampian urinals and graffiti, illustrating the fluid and

Fig. 1.10 New York County National Bank, New York, 2021. (Photograph courtesy Ferda Kolatan.)

Misfit conditions also occur in cohesive buildings. The skewed relationship between the miniaturized porticos, tall windows, and raised foundation walls creates intriguing tensions and misalignments in this example.

somewhat capricious nature of how art is delineated as such within a specific period by a particular society and its cultural institutions.

In their essay "When is Artification?," sociologists Roberta Shapiro and Nathalie Heinich define artification as "a dynamic process of social change through which new objects and practices emerge and relationships and institutions are transformed."[16] The emergence of new objects and practices resulting from social and cultural shifts is precisely what fuels our interest in misfits. Art (in this context, architecture) is not an inherent quality intrinsic to individual objects; rather, it is extrinsic and contingent upon the interplay of symbolic, material, and contextual factors.[17] It is vital to emphasize, however, that objects are not just the passive outcomes of the processes that shape them. On the contrary, they are implicitly engaged in *worldmaking* and have the capacity to instigate change in their own right. This dual nature of objects, as both manifestations of societal change and as semiautonomous entities capable of envisioning potential futures, renders them profoundly intriguing. However, understanding this duality also requires a delicate balancing act. Tipping too far to one side, the object risks being reduced to a mere symptom–an unproductive prospect for designers who bear the responsibility of shaping them. Swinging too far to the other side, however, the object may become a kind of fetish, privileging subjective viewpoints and potentially limiting its resonance within a broader society.

This delicate balancing act is embodied in the aesthetic attributes of misfit and hybrid architecture. Shapiro and Heinich go on to assert, "extracting or displacing a production from its initial context is a prerequisite for artification."[18] Their examples include film's transition from fairs to theaters, breakdancing's shift from the street to the stage, and graffiti's transformation through photography and publication in art books. These acts of decontextualization involving artistic media and institutions recall Shklovsky's notion of defamiliarization as a creative technique. Estrangement, it seems, pervades across various scales and domains, yet it remains inherently tied to *form*–whether expressed as text, object, architecture, medium, or institution.

The projects featured in this book have two distinct yet interconnected objectives. First, to direct attention toward misfits, and second, to recontextualize misfits through techniques of defamiliarization by extracting them from the obscure urban backdrop of non-architecture and placing them into a context that allows us to evaluate and regard them as architecture via hybridization. The three aesthetic concepts of calling-power, defamiliarization, and artification, coupled with the object's role as an agent balancing societal currents and its own autonomous capacity to engender change, establish the overarching framework for the conceptual and aesthetic attributes of hybrids.

NOTES

4   By "suppressed, forgotten, and fragmented storylines," I refer to material and cultural histories that are present in all built matter but are no longer legible, or were never meant to be legible, as is the case with most infrastructure or mundane standardized architectural components. The "storylines" are embodied by the misfits and thus reactivated in novel form. The aesthetic differences in the Cairo, Istanbul, and New York projects are to a large part due to the local techniques and protocols—or stories—that have produced the misfits.

5   In this context, "late-capitalist urban transformations" primarily refers to large-scale urban developments and renewal projects that result in jarring, misfit juxtapositions with preexisting districts with respect to scale, style, and class.

6   This notion of viewing the city as a collection of objects is partly inspired by Graham Harman's Object-Oriented Philosophy. For Harman, all objects are irreducible to their immaterial relationships with other objects and the world, as well as their internal material structure. While those conditions determine the physical properties of objects, they never fully exhaust their being. An unaccounted *reserve*, which Harman calls "withdrawnness," remains. It is from this reserve, according to Harman, that real change emerges. Applying this object-notion to the city at large flattens existing hierarchical dependencies and opens the way for new collaborative acts based on oblique affinities. For an in-depth account of Harman's object definitions, see: Graham Harman, *The Quadruple Object* (Winchester: Zero Books, 2011).

7   *Embodied carbon* is the energy and emissions associated with building materials, construction, and transportation, as opposed to *operational carbon*, which is the energy associated with warming, cooling, lighting, ventilating, and powering buildings. The World Green Building Council released a 2019 report stating, "As operational carbon is being reduced, embodied carbon will continue to grow in importance as a proportion of total emissions. While we must continue to focus on addressing operational carbon we must now rapidly increase efforts to tackle embodied carbon emissions at a global scale, too." The WGBC estimates global embodied carbon emissions at 11% (https://worldgbc.org/advancing-net-zero/embodied-carbon/). More recent estimations set the number at 13% (https://achitecture2030.org).

8   In the words of the 94th AIA president Carl Elefante, "the greenest building is the one that already exists." Robert Adam, "The greenest building is the one that already exists," *Architect's Journal*, September 24, 2019, https://www.architectsjournal.co.uk/news/opinion/the-greenest-building-is-the-one-that-already-exists. Or, as architect Larry Strain suggests, "reuse buildings instead of constructing new ones." Larry Strain, "10 steps to reducing embodied carbon," AIA, March 2017, https://www.aia.org/articles/70446-ten-steps-to-reducing-embodied-carbon.

9   One good example of this is the Rainbow Stairs in Istanbul. In 2013 a private citizen, Hüseyin Çetinel, took it upon himself to paint all 145 steps of a public staircase connecting the neighborhoods of Fındıklı and Cihangir in rainbow colors. Soon thereafter the stairs became a popular public artifact for people to gather around and further modify them with graffiti and other street art. The rainbow colors attracted nearby residents, tourists, and activists who were drawn by the color's affinity to the LGBTQ+ pride flag (Çetinel had originally chosen the colors simply "to make people smile"). Eventually, the local government felt threatened by the political innuendo associated with the stairs and painted them over in gray. After a public outcry, however, the stairs were reinstated in their rainbow colors.

10   This notion draws from what Jane Bennett calls "thing-power" or "the calling-power of things," the capacity of objects to "command attention, exude a kind of dignity, provoke poetry, or inspire fear." For Bennett, those qualities are an indication of the vitality of "things in their own right" and attribute to them a more active and privileged status than that of merely passive *stuff*. Jane Bennett, "The Force of Things: Steps Toward and Ecology of Matter," *Political Theory* 32, no. 3 (June 2004): 347–72.

11   Jane Bennett, "Powers of the Hoard: Artistry and Agency in a World of Vibrant Matter," Lecture, Vera List Center, September 24, 2011, https://vimeo.com/29535247.

12   There are, of course, more factors that determine aesthetic judgements of architectural objects. The list only mentions the most common criteria through which buildings' sensory qualities are assessed.

13   Viktor Shklovsky, "Art as Technique" in *Russian Formalist Criticism Four Essays*, ed. Lee T. Lemon and Marion J. Reis (Lincoln: University of Nebraska Press, 2012), 13.

14 The full passage reads: "The purpose of art is to impart the sensation of things as they are perceived and not as they are known. The technique of art is to make objects 'unfamiliar,' to make forms difficult, to increase the difficulty and length of perception because the process of perception is an aesthetic end in itself and must be prolonged." Shklovsky, "Art as Technique," 12.

15 Shklovsky, "Art as Technique," 12.

16 Roberta Shapiro and Nathalie Heinich, "When is Artification?," *Contemporary Aesthetics* 4 (2012), 2.

17 Shapiro and Heinich. "When is Artification?," 3.

18 Shapiro and Heinich. "When is Artification?," 5.

Hybrid Artifacts

In the realm of architecture, the allure of the hybrid's manifold and contradictory character was perhaps most poignantly articulated by Robert Venturi over half a century ago:

> *I like elements that are hybrid rather than "pure," compromising rather than "clean," distorted rather than "straightforward," ambiguous rather than "articulated," perverse as well as impersonal, boring as well as "interesting," conventional rather than "designed," accommodating rather than excluding, redundant rather than simple, vestigial as well as innovating, inconsistent and equivocal rather than direct and clear. I am for messy vitality over obvious unity.*[19]

The transformation of urban misfits into new hybrid artifacts is the central concern of this book. In the broadest sense, this transformation seizes on urban disparities and weaves them into new designs via techniques of extraction, combination, and fusion. While the work presented here shares Venturi's fascination with things "impure" and "vestigial," the techniques used to design hybrids are quite different. While hybrid artifacts retain a strong semblance to the original context from which they are pulled, they are subject to alterations: either through a gradual reshaping and reconfiguration of their inherent components or through the introduction and fusion of new elements. For instance, the peculiar misalignments and overlaps that have manifested over time and shaped the arched structure of an old Han in Istanbul are selectively extended, reimagined, and recombined into hybrid artifacts **(Fig. 1.11)**. Decorative elements, once scattered throughout the Han, such as tiling or window tracery, assume prominent roles within the artifact, blurring the distinction between ornamental and structural elements. It is the interaction between these elements–where and how they converge, their material and geometrical differences and affinities–that emerges as the central characteristic of hybrid design.

The term *artifact* encompasses a wide range of referents, including individual components, ornaments, infrastructure, landscapes, as well as buildings. Understood as an object with architectural qualities, rather than a building per se, the *artifact* resists predefined typological classifications. Moreover, the etymology of artifact implies its own hybrid composition, being both artificial and real (*ars factum*), reflecting our interest in the creation of *real fictions*. The term's common application in the field of archaeology also aligns with our approach, considering

Fig. 1.11 Ryan Henriksen & Tae Hyung, arch hybridization studies, renderings, Istanbul Studio, University of Pennsylvania Weitzman School of Design, 2019.

that hybrids are assembled in part from found or discovered objects within the urban depository. The seemingly paradoxical conditions of made and found, artificial and real, are omnipresent in the city, and precisely delineate the scope of our interest, making *artifact* an apt and suitable descriptor for our undertaking.

When it comes to the term *hybrid*, an even broader spectrum of referents and meanings awaits. In today's parlance, *hybrid* can refer to all kinds of societal, scientific, or artistic endeavors, underscoring the term's versatility and popularity. Originally rooted in biology, the *hybrid* has come to denote an entity that prioritizes combinatorial principles over notions of purity or essence.[20] Imaginary creatures like the Assyrian Lamassu, the Egyptian Sphinx, or the Satyrs, Centaurs, and Minotaur populating Greek mythologies point to a deep-seated fascination with the chimerical expressions of blended forms across history. While these hybrids were often viewed as unsettling anomalies, they also embodied positive qualities like strength, knowledge, courage, or power.

With the onset of industrialization in more modern times, technological hybrids began to proliferate, fusing machinic components with human and animal forms.[21] The contemporary iterations of these early technological hybrids–cyborgs, replicants, humanoids, and various other bionic creatures–have become staples in science-fiction narratives and indispensable to pop culture. But storytelling is not the only realm where hybrids thrive these days. Most visual arts, in particular music and fashion, have embraced unlikely assemblies crafted from disparate parts. This is evidenced by the creative use of increasingly sophisticated techniques in mixing, sampling, and cross-referencing aimed at creating novel forms, meaning, and aesthetic effects through unexpected combinations. In the sciences and engineering, hybrid technologies are also widely employed to enhance the effects, efficiency, and performance of a large variety of things including cars, drugs, computers, agriculture, and power plants.

Given the abundance and popularity of hybrids in so many fields, it is rather curious that architecture has remained somewhat indifferent to them. Of course, this is not the case with software packages, plugins, composite design materials, fabrication and construction techniques, or programmatic organization. In these arenas, the benefits of hybridization for architecture are pursued with enthusiasm. However, surprisingly little emphasis is placed on exploring the formal and aesthetic conditions that arise from these hybrid techniques and tactics. Perhaps, this reluctance is due to concerns that any architectural exploration in this direction may be susceptible to the same failures and regressive tendencies of past eclectic architecture, whether the historicism of the late 19th century or the postmodernism of the 1970s and '80s. Alternatively, to focus explicitly on appearance or aesthetics may be considered a superfluous deflection from the performative capabilities of hybrids. Whatever the reasons for this neglect, architects will miss an opportunity to fully harness the creative potential of hybrids unless they explore their full range of possibilities.

* * *

One might wonder why hybrids, in both concept and form, have such broad resonance across contemporary culture. At first glance, their allure might stem from our perception that they exist as outliers to the norms and conventions that govern our everyday lives. Much like misfits, hybrids possess the capacity to surprise and even shock audiences with their mixed and provocative nature.[22] This particular characteristic of hybrids, embodying dissent and acting as rebels of sorts, stands in a seeming contradiction to their other chief trait: representing broader cultural themes driven by pluralistic ideas and societal uncertainties. This confounding capacity to capture the larger trends of our time while still retaining the charm of the outsider distinguishes hybrids.

However, there is yet another aspect of hybrids that makes them particularly relevant in the context of our age. By inhabiting thresholds, boundaries, and intersections, and by forging improbable alliances across them, hybrids gradually erode the long-standing dichotomies that have fortified Western ideologies for centuries. Dualistic pairings like nature/culture, culture/technology, real/ideal, or ancient/modern have shaped worldviews and guided intellectual discourses since the Enlightenment era, molding societies not only in the West but across the globe. The pursuit of an unchanging "truth" or "real," more often than not, has led to these antinomies that solidify into axiomatic positions with rigid hierarchies, classifications, taxonomies, and rulesets.[23] As the adverse societal and ecological consequences of this paradigm–a world governed by irreconcilable opposites–

become undeniable, the necessity for alternative and more sensible thought models, characterized by nuance, mediation, and remedy becomes indisputable.[24]

The observation that modernity's attempt to capture the world within clearly defined boundaries poses a paradox was eloquently articulated by sociologist and anthropologist Bruno Latour.[25] According to Latour, the modern condition itself can be best understood as a kind of cross-categorical hybrid, which, in turn, is the consequence of a fundamental dilemma. On the one hand, he argues, modern society attempts to apprehend the world through scientific means. This process, referred to as "translation" by Latour, inevitably contaminates and alters what it attempts to apprehend via technological protocols, institutional culture, and political agency. On the other hand, modern society also delineates humans and nonhumans into two distinct and separate ontological categories, a process that Latour terms "purification."[26] The conflict between the notion of pure existential categories occupied either by nature or culture and the inevitable contamination of these categories through translation is what Latour refers to as the "modern paradox."[27]

NOTES

19   Robert Venturi, *Complexity and Contradiction in Architecture* (New York: Museum of Modern Art, 1966), 22.

20   The *Oxford English Dictionary* defines a *hybrid* as "the offspring of two animals or plants of different species or varieties; a half-breed, cross-breed, or mongrel." The negative connotations often associated with synonyms (racial slurs, notions of "impurity," etc.) point to a misguided yet deep-seated prejudice toward mixing as an act of dilution rather than enrichment and creativity as it is understood in the book.

21   The most famous literary example for a machine-human hybrid might be Mary Shelley's monster from her 1818 novel *Frankenstein; or the Modern Prometheus*. Shelley's tragic creature created an enduring Romantic metaphor for human transformation and alienation in the technological age. Her depiction of an ill-fated machine-human has served as an archetype for countless science-fiction interpretations, including such popular films as *Metropolis* (1927), *Blade Runner* (1982), and *Ex Machina* (2014).

22   One might recall here the Dadaist or Surrealist assemblages that left audiences in states of confusion or even anger, or the previously mentioned Frankensteinian monsters fashioned from disparate parts. Perhaps the closest we come to experiencing "shock" from hybrids in contemporary times is within the realm of genetic engineering and the ongoing advancements in Artificial Intelligence (AI), along with the bewildering prospects of a transhuman future.

23   I am referring here primarily to the Platonic and Aristotelian traditions, which have significantly influenced Western thought by establishing a metaphysical "real" populated by ideal forms, and by classifying nature into clearly definable categories.

24   The detrimental societal and ecological effects are evident in the transformation of these philosophies into rigid class structures and the objectification of the environment as a quantifiable entity.

25   Bruno Latour, *We Have Never Been Modern* (Cambridge: Harvard University Press, 1993).

26   Latour, *We Have Never Been Modern*, 10.

27   Latour, *We Have Never Been Modern*, 30.

From Parts to Objects

Having outlined the overarching ideas and motivations that underpin misfits and hybrid artifacts, we now turn to more specifically architectural inquiries. As indicated in the introduction, this book advocates for a shift in terminology from *parts* to *objects*. This shift is intended to loosen and reconfigure the inherent hierarchy in architectural conceptions of part-to-whole relationships. Such loosening is crucial to our pursuit of cultivating *odd* component relationships and fostering hybridization. Our interest in objects situates our endeavor within a rich disciplinary debate that has, over significant periods, laid the ideological groundwork for the production and assessment of architecture. If hybrids have indeed emerged as an expression of a paradigmatic cultural shift toward composite forms, it is imperative to scrutinize the influence of such hybridizations on our understanding of architectural assembly.

It remains an indisputable fact that all assemblies are beholden to some notion of part-to-whole organization. After all, a comprehensive understanding of the interaction between building parts is the prerequisite for successful planning and construction. The relational hierarchy that extends from a building down to its facades, bricks, windows, doors, frames, insulation, and hardware, etc. forms the most basic tenets of architectural practice. But what happens when the flow of this sequence of relations is inevitably interrupted due to age, dysfunction, poor planning, or mere happenstance? Can misfits still be reasonably classified as parts if they no longer contribute to a coherent or intentional whole? For instance, if a facade stands alone, as might occur during a gut renovation, does its significance still remain tied to its function as a part of a larger structure? Answering the latter question in the affirmative leads to an irrevocable conclusion: the facade has become dysfunctional, residing in a state of disrepair, awaiting rehabilitation and reintegration within the entirety of the building, or demolition.

But one could take a different position on the facade in this scenario, regarding it as having been liberated from its former relational dependencies, poised for fresh reinterpretation. Perhaps, a new configuration could be envisaged that does not hinge on the facade's definition as a part of a larger building envelope. Maybe, at this stage, the facade ceases to be a facade altogether, and simply becomes a rectangular plane made of red brick with a series of openings cut into it. Examining this object from both a conceptual and design standpoint would permit interventions that extend beyond those prescribed by the systematic definitions of buildings as unified wholes. It thus becomes possible to imagine an architecture where the

Fig. 1.12 Hybrid Artifacts, renderings, Istanbul Studio,
University of Pennsylvania Weitzman School of Design, 2018–19.

facade takes on entirely different roles, interacting with the street and the city in novel ways, and forging new relationships with elements like sidewalks, streetlights, or infrastructure (Fig. 1.13). This perceptual shift, from facade to planar object with apertures, deliberately undermines relational preconceptions to allow for an out-of-order reconfiguration and hybridization of components.

The example of the facade illustrates our approach, yet there is no set scale or functional limit dictating what can qualify as an object. A handrail, a window frame, a chimney, as well as ventilation towers, bridges, and drydocks all possess the potential for new hybrid roles once they are freed from relationships of subordination to a whole. The practice of redefining parts as objects is not, however, contingent on the malfunction or decay of the whole. Any component, intact or not, offers virtually the same opportunities for reappropriation as one that stands alone, exposed, and decontextualized. Consequently, the definition of a misfit is remarkably flexible, relying less on the condition of a specific part and more on its ability to inspire unscripted collaborative acts of design.

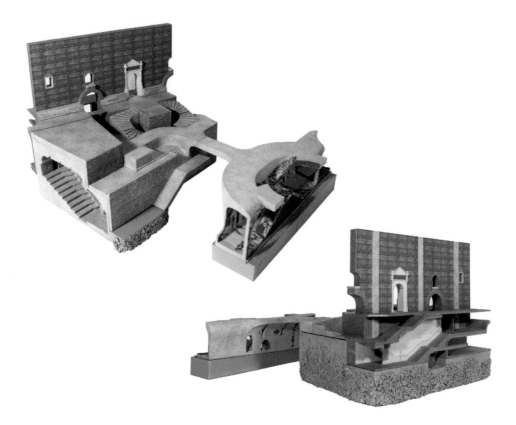

Fig. 1.13 Carla Bonilla & Yang Li & Neera Sharma, Tophane, powder-print model, Istanbul Studio, University of Pennsylvania Weitzman School of Design, 2018.

The facade of a historic Ottoman armory in Istanbul, its elevated base, and an adjacent tram station have been modeled as individual objects forming a semiautonomous ensemble, from which new urban spaces and programmatic entwinements emerge.

Hybridization necessitates a degree of equality among the elements it incorporates. If these elements are organized within functional hierarchical structures, they are less likely to encourage material intersections beyond their inherent structural and organizational confines. Object-to-object relationships, contrary to part-to-whole, privilege a different ethic regarding the interplay of architectural and urban elements. All buildings and infrastructure undergo transformations over time that yield leftovers, misalignments, and residues that are no longer legible as parts but still retain their identity as objects. To perceive these conditions as opportunities for design rather than simply urban fallout is the first step of hybridization.

The philosopher Graham Harman eloquently expounds on this de-hierarchized view of the material world. In Harman's formulation, objects are not necessarily self-centered entities completely devoid of relations or hierarchies, isolated from the forces and agencies that shape society. Rather, for Harman, objects are equally enmeshed within the myriad networks that define and structure the world. The distinction lies in the conceit that they possess a degree of autonomy, enabling them to disentangle themselves from these networks and establish fresh alliances, often unexpectedly. According to Harman, these alliances, rather than reinforcing rigid hierarchical systems in which some objects are subsumed by their relations to others, form yet other objects.[28] Contemplating architectural relations and hierarchies as endlessly expandable and variable constellations of objects is an invigorating exercise, in tune with the hybrid's ambiguous nature and its inherent propensity for perpetual reconfiguration.

A notion of object-to-object relations stands in stark contrast to the idealizations of part-to-whole hierarchies deep-seated in Western culture. When Vitruvius wrote in the 1st century BCE of the "proper agreement between the members of the work itself," he echoed ideas reaching back to Greek antiquity that sought to align architecture with what were thought to be the fundamental laws of nature.[29] Nature, following this tradition, is understood as an elaborate system of parts operating in harmony, governed by eternal rules, and manifested through an intricate set of hierarchical proportions and symmetries. These hierarchies are thus the embodiments of natural laws rather than mere features, not only manifesting the material world (nature) but infusing it with intangible values such as beauty, justice, and truth.[30] This fusion of part-to-whole aesthetics with broader convictions about truth and reality became a foundational characteristic of the European architectural canon in the subsequent centuries.

Alberti provided one of the most enduring and poignant part-to-whole definitions, characterizing it as "the harmony and concord of all the parts achieved in such a manner that nothing could be added or taken away or altered except for the worse."[31] This maxim, delivered during the Renaissance, encapsulates classical ideals and has persisted as a guiding compositional principle for architecture into the 21st century. In many ways, the lineage of Vitruvian and Albertian conceptions of part-to-whole relations, centered around unity and perfection achieved through harmoniously orchestrated components, has become ideologically hardwired into the profession. This fact, however, does not preclude the opposition to the rigid orthodoxy of these ideas that accompanied them. Mannerist distortions and Baroque concatenation stretched and challenged the definitions of perfect harmony, giving rise to new stylistic forms with distinct ideological orientations. But they never fully broke with their precedent.

Even 20th-century Classical Modernism, which remains a globally influential force in architecture to this day (in contrast to Postmodernism, which has more or less been relegated to the annals of history), embarked on a quest for the "correct" form of composition.[32] Its departure, in many instances, from literal anthropomorphism characterized by axial symmetries toward a more abstract machine aesthetic represents a primarily metaphorical shift in considerations of part-to-whole relationships, rather than a complete renunciation of their core principles. Perhaps, Deconstructivism, following the tail end of Postmodernism and sharing the same linguistic preoccupations, could be considered as the most significant attempt to radically divorce architecture from prevailing ideologies of part-to-whole.[33] However, this movement, owing to its brevity, the diverse range of work it aimed to encompass, and the limited and exclusive group of architects associated with it, was unable to make a comprehensive or enduring impact on the field.

The advent of digital technology in architecture has introduced its own spin on the concept of part-to-whole. Here, *parts* became entirely absorbed into larger behavioral systems and networks, acting primarily as quantitative nodes or parametric units with binary functions, devoid of meaning outside the system itself. The ideological aspirations vested in the hierarchical interplay of parts and wholes gave way to an ethic of *performance*, according to which success is measured by adaptability and variability.[34] In this respect, the digital paradigm appears to distinguish itself from earlier paradigms that aimed to establish immutable truths. This focus on performance and break from earlier part-to-whole hierarchies does not mean, however, that the digital approach foregoes the broader ideological tendencies of the discipline. Through its customary references to natural forces, dynamic fields, and genetic codes, etc., and its biomorphic aesthetics, the digital paradigm aligns more closely with classical conceptions of architecture as a vehicle for representing "real" nature than one might initially assume.

This brief historical overview of part-to-whole relationships and their role in shaping and reflecting broader cultural ideas aims to highlight both parallels and disparities between hybrid architecture and existing models. Our object-to-object approach rejects ideologies that prioritize dogmatic sentiments of right and wrong, truth and falsehood, beauty and ugliness, and challenges their zero-tolerance stance on variation and aberrance. However, the conceptual reorganization of hierarchically structured parts into semiautonomous objects also diverges markedly from the digital paradigm's tendency to subordinate its parts to an all-powerful system. Postmodernism's play with signification through decontextualization and combinatorial techniques shares obvious similarities with hybridization, yet it differs in its reliance on disciplinary knowledge, historical precedent, and language to effectively convey its message.

Hybrid artifacts aim to cultivate an entirely distinct ideology, or even an *anti-ideology*, wherein the pluralistic tendencies of contemporary culture find embodiment in the diversity of urban and architectural elements, irrespective of their scale, type, origin, or perceived significance. By designating and treating these elements as equal objects, liberated from preconceived hierarchies, they acquire an autonomy that enables cross-categorical alliances and mergers, while retaining the imprints of their own material and cultural histories. These histories are viewed as tangible features of the objects, rather than immaterial forces that establish hierarchies and instantiate new systems of order and value. The value derived from object-to-object relationships emerges from unexpected and often unlikely affinities that draw them together. What is thus primarily represented by the depository of objects, and in hybrid architecture, is the full potential of the city, in all of its transitory or contradictory attributes, and their capacity to produce design in accidental or pedestrian acts of collaboration.

NOTES

28 Harman also includes the beholder as an inseparable constituent in his definition of objects. According to Harman, the beholder and the objects being beheld form tertiary entities that cannot be reduced to their individual constituents. These human/nonhuman hybrids suggest new ontological perspectives and challenge models that privilege anthropocentric views. Graham Harman, *Art and Objects* (Cambridge: Polity Press, 2020), 173.

29 Vitruvius, *The Ten Books on Architecture*, trans. Morris Hicky Morgan (Cambridge: Harvard University Press, 1914), 14.

30 This tradition is largely rooted in Pythagoras's notion of the "Harmony of the Spheres" and Plato's concept of forms, both of which unify beauty, justice, and truth within an idealized cosmology.

31 Rudolf Wittkower, *Architectural Principles in the Age of Humanism* (London: Alec Tiranti Ltd., 1952), 29.

32 One might think here of Le Corbusier's famous statement: "Architecture is the masterly, correct and magnificent, play of masses brought together in light." Le Corbusier, *Towards A New Architecture* (New York: Dover Publications, Inc., 1986), 29.

33 In his introduction to the catalogue of the 1988 "Deconstructivist Architecture" exhibition at MoMA, Mark Wigley describes the exhibited projects as "offering a different sensibility" compared to classical architecture, "one in which the dream of pure form has been disturbed. Form has become contaminated. The dream has become a kind of nightmare." Philip Johnson and Mark Wigley, eds., *Deconstructivist Architecture* (New York: MoMA, 1988), 10.

34 This is evidenced by the industry's utilization of digital techniques primarily for performance-driven building elements like curtain walls or structural systems, which rely on the controllability of parts and the ability of the system to "respond" within a set range of functional parameters.

Another Kind
of Architectural Fantasy

Hybrid artifacts exist at the intersection of reality, conjecture, and fabulation. They identify perceived idiosyncrasies and incompatibilities inherent in cities and weave them into architectural fictions. Some of these fictions are straightforward, practical, and actionable, while others are intricate and speculative, primarily intended to tease open our imagination. Often, both of these qualities coexist within a single project. Hybrids unfold as urban character studies of sorts–playful yet inquisitive, casting a light upon the city's often overlooked and unexplored material accumulations and juxtapositions.

After having outlined the environmental and sociocultural benefits and aesthetic characteristics of hybrids and articulated how their object-to-object relationships subvert previous part-to-whole conceptions, one final task remains. Hybrid artifacts must be situated within a genre of architectural representation, not only to frame their disciplinary contributions and enhance their credibility but also because, in the spirit of mixing and meshing, they have indeed drawn inspiration from older precedents. As our artifacts are meant to visualize hybrid design as a form of *real fiction*–rather than deliver detailed drawings for executing it–they should be considered in the tradition of the architectural fantasy drawing.

Since the days of the Renaissance, the fantasy drawing has served as a unique medium for contemplating the meaning of architecture, and has proven to be an invaluable tool for design inquiry and experimentation. As historian John Wilton-Ehly articulates, "architectural fantasy in paintings, drawings and engravings had also a creative function, as an outlet for artists' and architects' imaginative expression or experiments, uninhibited by the prescriptive terms of commissions or by practical needs."[35] While the absence of external constraints grants creative freedom when exploring architecture, it also allows for a more focused examination of a particular era's interests and preoccupations.

Architectural fantasy is in many ways an artistic response to collective psychological needs, which are less likely to be reflected by an architecture constrained by "real-world" factors such as budgets, schedules, codes, and so forth. Notions like *unrealistic* or *improbable*, which often characterize fantasy, should thus be understood from a nuanced perspective. The architecture depicted in fantasy drawings is deemed unrealistic mainly because it has not been realized in the

Fig. 1.14 Amber Farrow
& Molly Zmich, Stair Artifact,
rendering, New York Studio,
University of Pennsylvania
Weitzman School of Design, 2021.

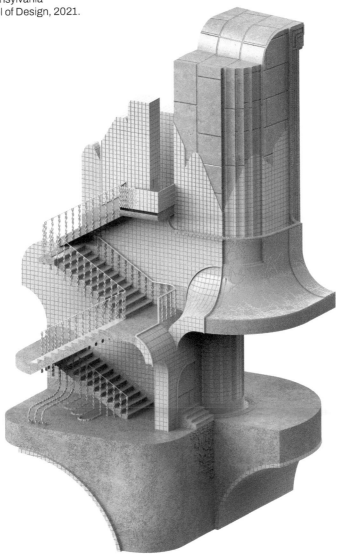

form of executed buildings. However, these fantasies are unquestionably *real* as
ideas and representations of authentic psychological and cultural aspirations. The
architectural fantasies embodied by hybrid artifacts reside within this domain.
Moreover, hybrids exhibit specific compositional and aesthetic attributes consistent
with certain predecessors, two of which we will examine more closely.

The Capriccio

The first precedent bearing affinities to the hybrid artifact is the capriccio, a genre that gained prominence in the 18th century through Italian artists like Giovanni Paolo Panini, Canaletto, and Piranesi. Described by Wilton-Ehly as "a drawing or painted or engraved composition combining features of imaginary and/or real architecture, ruined or intact, in a picturesque setting," the capriccio introduced fantastical and whimsical scenes into the realms of landscape and architectural painting.[36] Reflecting an epoch engrossed in archaeology and antiquity, the capriccio frequently depicted fictionalized Roman ruins scattered across picturesque landscapes. However, capriccios illustrating peculiar urban arrangements were also common and hold greater relevance to our discussion. One such example is Giovanni Paolo Panini's 1729 *Piazza Navona*, in which the piazza's existing structures are complemented by an array of fictitious elements like monumental columns, arches, and altars. The resulting ensemble, envisioned by the painter as a grand display of architectural symbols, today strikes us as an eccentric sequence of decontextualized architectural fragments and curious juxtapositions. Since Panini's elements do not physically intersect, they are not true hybrids as we define them. However, upon closer inspection, one notices a continuous base beneath the new additions, implying that the components form a larger composite. This assemblage of objects, akin to a misfit, registers an urban quality stressing the frictions and perplexing effects of dissimilar adjacent objects, rather than amplifying the spatial properties of the piazza.

Another example worth mentioning is the famous *Carceri* etchings by Piranesi.[37] Produced approximately three decades after the *Piazza Navona*, the *Imaginary Prisons* series displays a markedly different character and mood from Panini's painting.[38] With an aura of brooding darkness, claustrophobia, and intricacy, the *Carceri* depict a somber vision of the city's hidden underbelly. An explicitly mundane collection of unembellished structural and mechanical components, including pillars, beams, buttresses, stairs, ramps, ladders, drawbridges, chains, pulleys, guardrails, and lanterns, converge into improbable labyrinthine designs. The narratives of the *Carceri* unfold not through heroic gestures or nostalgically picturesque landscapes adorned with ancient ruins, but rather through deceptive and severe compositions that portend the industrial age. The distinction between exterior and interior dissolves, ground and sky are rendered unintelligible, and perspective varies with each etching. The cumulative effect is one of disorientation, disbelief, and tension. Despite their far less somber disposition, hybrids involve a similar cross-hatching of mundane parts.

Another crucial facet of the capriccio, further accentuating its importance as a precedent of hybrid artifacts, is its ability to conjure complex new narratives from the intermingling of diverse architectural and cultural themes. Lucien Steil touches upon this aspect, noting, "the architectural capriccio addresses the invention of buildings and space, cities, and landscapes and the multiply layered relationships between buildings and spaces, city and countryside, history and politics, people and places, and so on, through a variety of narratives, images and scales, and within a dense metaphysical and mythological complexity."[39] While the capriccio's capacity to craft "multiply layered relationships" and imbue images with "meta-physical and mythological" undertones might appear quaint in today's bustling urban landscape, it serves as a reminder of our deep-seated inclination to infuse inanimate objects with meaning and maintain a visceral and spiritual closeness to them. In an era when the chasm between us and our physical environment seems ever widening, and the division between subject and object, human and nonhuman, grows more pronounced, architecture's intrinsic ability to bridge these divides and chart alternative trajectories becomes essential.

The Rocaille

The rocaille is the hybrids closest historical relative. Originating in Louis XV's France during the early part of the 18th century, this versatile and intriguing aesthetic tradition epitomizes many of the concepts, techniques, and aesthetic aspirations of hybrids. As the foundation of the Rococo style, the rocaille is the central motif seen across etchings, paintings, household objects, furniture, interiors, and buildings. Initially conceived as an abstract illustration, free from concerns of scale, structural functionality, and technical or ideological part-to-whole relationships, the rocaille offers a remarkably flexible template for various design applications. Defined by Fiske Kimball as "rock-work and shellwork for the incrustation of grottoes and fountains," the rocaille is rooted in the decorative.[40] Highly ornate, with a predilection for asymmetrical composition and whimsical amalgamations of rocks, shells, scrolls, pediments, volutes, and other bits tectonic and organic, the rocaille, and consequently the Rococo, has been dismissed by critics and historians as insincere and frivolous. It was often seen as a confusing "dynamic unity of ensembles" that deviated from "older artistic prejudices in favor of purity of self-contained elements."[41]

The Rococo was considered an affront to the foundational principles of architecture, while the rocaille emerged as a *means* to "obscure constructive effort," to veil what truly held significance in building–namely, its discernible structural and symbolic arrangements.[42] This sentiment is eloquently captured by Christopher Tadgell: "in this [Rococo] mode the Orders had no place–or they were invaded, eaten away and undermined by naturalistic or stylized floral motifs in a mockery of their claim to express the forces implicit in structure."[43] Unsurprisingly, these recalcitrant tendencies endear the rocaille to our cause as they challenged the ruling principles of their day and align, in our estimation, closer with object-to-object relationships than a part-to-whole hierarchy. Shrouding structural forces and symbolic orders by overlaying columns, walls, and ceilings with continuous stucco embellishments, the architecture of the rocaille eludes subservience to a hierarchically legible whole. Instead, it creates a unified, immersive aesthetic where all elements, whether decorative, structural, or symbolic, either blend harmoniously or exist in abrupt adjacencies, all simultaneously.

Often bound in illustrative collections intended for widespread replication and distribution, the rocaille not only revealed its shifty and contradictory nature but also enhanced its allure for a broader audience.[44] In the skilled engravings of artists like Jean Mondon and Juste-Aurèle Meissonnier, the interplay between real and abstract elements occurs in the context of fictional scenes of courtship, passion, melancholy, and other distinctly human fixations (Fig. 1.15). The psychological tensions playing out between human figures are mirrored in the asymmetries and strange constellations of the rocaille. Its treatment of both the natural and tectonic as equally legitimate, and the intimate entwinement of these elements with human actions and emotions, imbues the centuries-old rocaille with a strangely contemporary relevance. As such, the rocaille, much like the hybrid, exists in contrast to aesthetic traditions based on rigid categorical boundaries.

To highlight the capriccio and the rocaille as our precedents is, admittedly, a selective and somewhat reductive approach. After all, as we progress into the 20th century, hybridization becomes pervasive. The 20th century saw the emergence of artistic techniques such as collage, montage, assemblage, or bricolage, among others, emerge rapidly, all involving compositions crafted from unlikely fragments, components, and objects. In architecture, collage became integral to the fantasy

Fig. 1.15 Antoine Aveline (after Jean Mondon), *Le Rendez-vous*, etching, 1736. (Image courtesy Katherine Shepard Fund.)

This etching features a picturesque rocaille fountain, incorporating various C and S-scrolls. The fountain is the centerpiece around which a romantic scene unfolds. The rocaille orchestrates a mutual entwinement between humans and inanimate objects, becoming an active part of the narrative rather than its mere background.

drawing, particularly during the postwar years, when it was often used to depict political utopias and convey social commentary within avant-garde circles.[45] Contrarily, hybrid artifacts do not aspire to grand utopian visions prescribing wholesale societal change. They explicitly refrain from such confident convictions and declarations, focusing instead on the here and now. Change, for the hybrid, is a rather persistent force that can be tapped into, diverted, and gradually shaped to align with our interests and needs.

Hybrid artifacts are thus close in spirit to the capriccio or rocaille, as they innovate from within their respective domains. Rather than discarding old or disparate elements, they undergo meticulous study, drawing, modeling, amendment, and representation, resulting in fresh and novel forms. These artifacts avoid grand symbolic gestures, formal abstractions, or overreliance on specialized discourse, ensuring their accessibility to a wider audience. The fantasy conjured by hybrid artifacts is intricately woven from the existing fabric of the city, assuring that the hybrid's multiple references remain readily discernible. The observer's attention is drawn to the material world, fostering a sense of intimacy and direct engagement with it.

NOTES

35   John Wilton-Ehly, "Capriccio," Oxford Art Online, January 2004, https:// doi.org/10.1093/ gao/9781884446054.article.T013901.

36   Wilton-Ehly, "Capriccio," Oxford Art Online.

37   Giovanni Battista Piranesi's *Le Carceri d'Invenzione (The Imaginary Prisons)*, were issued in a set of 16 etchings between 1749 and 1761.

38   The etchings do not represent prisons in a literal sense. While some of them have titles like *The Man on the Rack*, the images mostly depict exaggerated yet generic manufactured spaces that represent the proto-industrial city by foregrounding its mechanical and structural members.

39   Lucien Steil, preface to *The Architectural Capriccio, Memory, Fantasy and Invention*, ed. Lucien Steill (London and New York: Routledge, 2014), liii.

40   Fiske Kimball, *The Creation of the Rococo* (New York: W.W. Norton & Company, Inc., 1964), 3.

41   Kimball goes on to suggest that this moral prejudice is rooted in the conflation of artistic qualities with the prevalent conception of morality of the period, according to which they were perceived as "corrupt" and "frivolous." Kimball, *The Creation of the Rococo*, 9.

42   Henry Russel-Hitchcock quotes Phillipe Minguet: "the Rococo plays at obscuring constructive effort". Henry Russel-Hitchcock, *Rococo Architecture in Southern Germany* (London: Phaidon Press, 1968), 15.

43   Christopher Tadgell, "France," in *Baroque & Rococo: Architecture & Decoration*, ed. Anthony Blunt (Hertfordshire: Wordsworth Editions, 1988), 134.

44   The rocaille was often developed independently from specific projects and published in collections or folios of printed illustrations. As such, they served as templates for other artisans and architects, who would integrate them into their work and create spinoffs. These collections allowed for a wider distribution and provided an affordable way to attain access to the work of masters. Coinciding with the rise of an affluent middle-class (bourgeoisie) in Europe, the Rococo became the first art form no longer contingent on the goodwill and patronage of the aristocracy. The subjects depicted in the rocaille reflect this by catering more strongly toward interests associated with everyday life.

45   Examples for this are numerous and include works by Superstudio, Archigram, Hans Hollein, Rem Koolhaas, and others.

ISTANBUL

Fig. 2.1 Zehua Zhang, Nusretiye Mosque, rendering,
Istanbul Studio, University of Pennsylvania Weitzman School of Design, 2018.

The Nusretiye Mosque and its surroundings exemplify the stylistic mashups that abound in Istanbul, where Ottoman, Baroque, Rococo, Neoclassical, and Modern elements often blend into unique hybrid expressions. Constructed between 1822 and 1826 by Armenian-Ottoman architect Krikor Balyan, the mosque reflects a desire to bridge Eastern and Western traditions. The project proposes a pavilion in the interstitial space between the mosque and the Tophane Kasrı (kiosk), designed by British architect William James Smith in 1852. The pavilion integrates architectural details from both structures, emphasizing and further estranging the site's eclectic character.

Istanbul

Unscripted Immediacies of Past, Present, and Future

From its beginnings as a small Greek settlement in the 6th century BCE to its rise as the capital of the Roman, Byzantine, and Ottoman empires, and its current state as the thriving cosmopolitan center of modern-day Turkey, Istanbul has been shaped by diverse and at times antagonistic forces.[46] Throughout history, the city's unique geographical location at the crossroads of Asia and Europe and along the banks of the Bosphorus strait that connects the Black Sea with the Mediterranean made it a coveted military stronghold for governing the larger region. Alongside these strategic advantages, Istanbul has a long history as an important artery for international trade, commercial enterprise, and cultural exchange. Linked to the region's various maritime and land-based trading routes since the days of Alexander the Great, Istanbul served as a converging point for traveling traders, merchants, and artisans spanning from Europe to the Arabian Peninsula and from the Mediterranean to the Asian steppes.[47]

It should come as no surprise, then, that Istanbul presents a particularly compelling case regarding misfit and hybrid architecture. As a melting pot of civilizations reaching back millennia, the city's DNA is steeped in the intersection, integration, and exchange of disparate ideas, customs, and cultural traditions. Any attempt to disentangle and purify these processes and histories into neat, singular categories from which to extract select elements and shape a grand, ordered narrative, or recover lost origins–be they real or mythic–misses the mark on what makes a city like Istanbul unique in the first place.

Marked by radical and, at times, violent historical transformations, Istanbul exemplifies both *disjunction* and *continuity*, which have left their conflicting traces along its streets and occasionally even on individual buildings and other urban structures. The work in this section explores these aspects of the city's rich heritage by devising propositions for select buildings and sites that, in some fashion, embody the curious tensions arising between disjunction and continuity.

Four simple yet crucial guidelines were applied in the development of the designs. Firstly, all projects began with a meticulous modeling of the sites, buildings, and their components, with a distinct focus on expressing details, textures, and colors to the fullest. These models encompassed both the intentional qualities of the original buildings and sites as well as those resulting from alterations, additions, accidents, and aging. This approach stands in stark contrast to more conventional methods that prioritize programmatic considerations and site analyses as the departure points for architectural design processes. Here, however, modeling is used as a tool for detecting and visualizing the more subtle and accidental qualities of a site's material conditions that are impossible to capture by means of program, function, or any kind of statistical and descriptive analysis.

Moreover, by modeling *everything*, including seemingly insignificant details, the projects avoid or at least minimize preconceived notions of the significance of a specific site or building based on original intentions or historical lineage. The thorough representation of built elements in all their various aspects and conditions reveals precisely the kind of diversified stories and histories that are suppressed in more conventional analyses. By diminishing the emphasis on original intentions and historical lineage as the primary means of assessing the significance of existing architecture, the models allow the many unscripted immediacies that characterize Istanbul to take center stage.

The second guideline focuses on how material objects–whether architectural, infrastructural, or organic–interact with each other. These interactions are particularly relevant for objects that are considered incompatible based either on their function, history, style, or perceived value. By acknowledging the formal and functional anomalies among the objects that comprise the built environment, and seeking design methodologies to incorporate them, conditions viewed as *incongruent* or *mismatched* become essential in the creation of new hybrid architecture. By the same token, identifying *unfitting* constellations within seemingly cohesive buildings, especially those considered iconic landmarks, challenges the prevailing notion that architectural value is contingent on the legibility of buildings as complete and original wholes.

All buildings, regardless of their age or significance, exhibit inconsistencies of some kind—moments where parts or objects collide unexpectedly and oddly. These conditions are potentially as significant to design as the planned and coordinated actions of architects and builders. Doing so not only expands the definition of architectural design but also leads to the *democratization* of the objects and conditions that come together in order to make a building.[48] Consequently, the focus on the perceived incompatibility of objects and the ways in which they converge becomes a crucial question for hybrid architecture.

The third guideline pertains to the modeling process itself. Once a misfit is identified, a digital model is created based on a series of detailed photographs. Creating a three-dimensional model from a photograph deviates significantly from the traditional practice of extrapolating three-dimensional forms from plans and sections or deriving them from conceptual massing models. In this approach, however, the model emerges from the peculiarities and inconsistencies captured in the photograph. The model is subsequently refined and expanded into a larger artifact or assembly.

Importantly, the model only incorporates elements that exist at the actual building or site or hold cultural relevance to the city. As a result, all shapes, details, textures, and colors in the initial model (and later in the finished artifact) possess qualities that are recognizable as belonging to the place. However, by emphasizing moments of incongruity and tension, these sensual qualities also appear estranged, decontextualized, and difficult to categorize. Once finalized into a hybrid artifact, the model must resemble a cohesive whole in seeming contradiction to the diverse and sometimes conflicting origins of its composition. The reason for this lies in the intrinsic distinction between hybrids and assemblages, and relates back to the second guideline. By carefully *fusing* disparate parts, textures, and colors, hybrids appear formally unified, as if their disparate elements were always intended to complete the whole. In contrast to assemblages, by downplaying the seams and boundaries between individual elements, hybrid artifacts defy straightforward dissection or classification.

As entities existing between the real and the imaginary, hybrid artifacts are neither meant to be regarded as building documents nor as purely utopian imaginings. Instead, they embody an intricate intertwining of the actual conditions of the site with the imaginative aspects arising from the combinatorial techniques employed in hybrid design.

The fourth and final guideline stipulates that the hybrid's multiple ambiguities must be supported by two visual formats. In the first, artifacts are portrayed as decontextualized objects floating on white backgrounds.[49] In these depictions, the city is presented as the kaleidoscopic reservoir of misfit conditions that gives rise to the hybrids. The relationships between the artifacts and their surroundings seem disconnected, but they are reflected in the hybridizations that incorporate and fuse together bits and pieces from their environment. This view renders quotidian urban conditions as potentially unique, even precious. The second format presents the artifacts fully integrated in their environment. These renderings and rendered photomontages employ a full-bleed, photorealistic style designed to immerse the viewer, in contrast to the distancing effect created by the floating objects. The combination of these formats expresses the conceptual and experimental nature of the hybrid artifacts and their ambition to offer realistic solutions.

Organized into four subchapters, the Istanbul projects encompass various sites, scales, and urban conditions, all with the aim of exploring hybrid architecture. The first subchapter, "Unlikely Affinities," serves as an introduction and warm-up exercise for the subsequent site-specific projects. This section comprises a series of photographs and modeled artifacts placed side by side, highlighting a fundamental principle of hybrid design: the identification of intriguing material relationships and their utilization in the creation of new forms of architecture. By documenting the unlikely affinities in the city's existing built environment, the groundwork is laid for the combinatorial processes from which hybrid artifacts are produced.

"Ambiguous Architecture" contemplates the interplay and boundaries between architectural objects that are perceived as either ordinary or extraordinary. The concept of the architectural icon is explored in terms of its potential for reinvention and acquiring new meaning and function. This subchapter explores the coexistence of the past and present in physical form and the blending of the quotidian with the exceptional. Arising from the tensions of these contrasting relationships are opportunities to reassess how the cultural significance of architecture–and the value it offers to its users–is determined.

The third subchapter, titled "Withdrawn Landmark," focuses on a historical han lying hidden in the dense fabric of Istanbul's crowded bazaar district. Recognizing and capitalizing on the han's incongruity within its present context, the projects in this subchapter grant the two-story structure a fresh programmatic and aesthetic identity. The Han's various transformations demonstrate how landmarked structures can be reintegrated into the contemporary life of the city through alternatives to the conventional approaches to historical preservation.

Finally, "Machinic Garden" uses the storied Imperial Ottoman shipyard as a case study to explore alternative approaches to the revitalization of valuable waterfront properties. Dismissing the conventional approach to urban renewal that prioritizes economic viability, the projects in this section examine how a former industrial site can give rise to new hybrid forms that seamlessly integrate mechanical devices and organic matter in unexpected and innovative ways. These hybrids represent broader inquiries regarding the role of technology and nature in the era of the Anthropocene.

NOTES

46   Beginning as a small Greek settlement known as Byzantium, Istanbul became an important trading location in late antiquity. In 330 CE, Emperor Constantine moved the empire's seat from Rome to the shores of the Bosphorus and renamed the city Constantinople. After a long siege in 1453, the Ottoman Turks under Fatih Sultan Mehmet conquered Constantinople and gave it the name Istanbul. The city served as the capital of the Ottoman Empire until its dissolution in 1922. Although Ankara became the official capital of the modern Turkish republic in 1923, Istanbul maintained and expanded its status as Turkey's cultural and commercial center.

47   Istanbul was an important city within the wide-stretching Silk Road network. The city served as a gateway for Europe to connect with the trading routes to the Middle and Far East.

48   Here, I use the term *democratization* in a nod to Levi Bryant, who argues for a flat realist ontology (which he terms "Onticology") in which all objects are neither reducible nor transcendent but defined by their dynamic interactions with each other. Levi R. Bryant, *The Democracy of Objects* (London: Open Humanities Press, 2011).

49   The physical models, which are made from 3-D color powder prints, also fall into this category as they are fabricated from the decontextualized objects models.

Unlikely Affinities

This subchapter focuses on the unheralded and obscure architectural moments that Istanbul produces with seeming effortlessness. On every corner, countless components meet and mingle in odd configurations, creating intriguing yet often overlooked architectural exhibits. The term *affinity* describes an attractive force, or sympathy, between substances.[50] The city, throughout the following section, is portrayed in episodes of conglomeration, moments or forms drawn together by an unanticipated attraction between disparate architectural and non-architectural elements. Here, the juxtaposition of photographs and hybrid artifacts alludes to our perception of the city as an immersive background from which certain conditions call our attention and become foregrounded.

What distinguishes architecture from other visual arts has traditionally been considered its spatial dimension.[51] Unlike painting, and to a lesser degree sculpture, architecture unfolds and expands through movement in space. However, I would argue that the most immediate way of experiencing architecture is predominantly as an image. A layperson walking about the city is more likely to pick up and respond to a building's external features–its facade or a particular ornament–than to the psychological, aesthetic, or political effects produced by the experience of its particular organization of space. This is not to diminish the importance and validity of these effects or to suggest that architecture perceived as image has no bearing on the politics of space, of course it does, but rather to acknowledge that our daily interactions with urban architecture are significantly influenced by what we see in front of us.

Foremost, "Unlikely Affinities" is a playful demonstration of how oddities captured in photographs can inspire new architectural objects. In the series of pairings of photographs and hybrid artifacts, Istanbul's architectural value is located in its ability to produce curious details, leftover pieces, and awkward additions. Together the photographs and artifacts comprise a kind of urban mood board, highlighting the incongruous architectural details that go largely unnoticed, overshadowed by a building's more dominant and easily discernible features.

While the photographs index real conditions, the artifacts register the sensual qualities of place and culture as architectural fictions. Without a specific site, scale, function, or program, the relationship between the artifacts and the realities depicted in the photographs is deliberately opaque. Some of the artifacts have more discernible ties to their photographic counterparts, while others offer only a remote semblance based on geometry, texture, or color. Even though the hybrid artifacts are reconfigurations of existing material conditions, the photographs do not provide exact templates or blueprints for their design. Rather, the relationship between image and object is based on *affinities*. At times, the artifacts incorporate elements from buildings that are not shown in the photograph or conjure novel elements by merging individual components. The goal of this exercise is to develop a dialogue between architecture-as-image and architecture-as-object without a hierarchically weighted direction or preference. To further accentuate the symbiotic relationship between image and object, some of the photographs have been paired with their respective artifacts after the fact.

This ambiguous correlation between image and object seizes on architecture's capacity to perform simultaneously as background and foreground. In which of these two states we happen to encounter architecture is contingent not simply on proximity or orientation but on the attention it commands or, in other words, how it strikes us as noteworthy or special in some capacity. Unsurprisingly, foregrounded buildings are usually considered more significant to our experience of the city, while misfit architecture tends to recede into the background, often overlooked as a kind of visual noise. The artifacts in this section offer a counternarrative by drawing out these concealed or veiled elements and foregrounding them in precious, one of a kind, objects. The coupling of photographs and artifacts reflects the city's constant oscillation between background and foreground.

NOTES

50 According to Merriam-Webster, the term *affinity* is typically used to describe sympathy among communities, such as kinship, friendship, and marriage, or between people and things. However, for our purposes, the term is extended to encompass all things and their interactions or assembly, to refer to likeness or to emphasize other connections between objects.

51 An example of this is the renowned German historian August Schmarsow's description of architecture's essence as the "making of space" (*Raumgestaltung*) and the "will to space" (*Raumwille*), linking it to what he determines as the natural human urge to move forward in space. August Schmarsow, *Barock und Rokoko: Eine Kritische Auseinandersetzung Über Das Malerische In Der Architecktur* (Leipzig: Verlag von S. Hirzel, 1897).

Figs. 2.2, 2.3

Figs. 2.4, 2.5

Figs. 2.6, 2.7

Figs. 2.8, 2.9

Figs. 2.10, 2.11

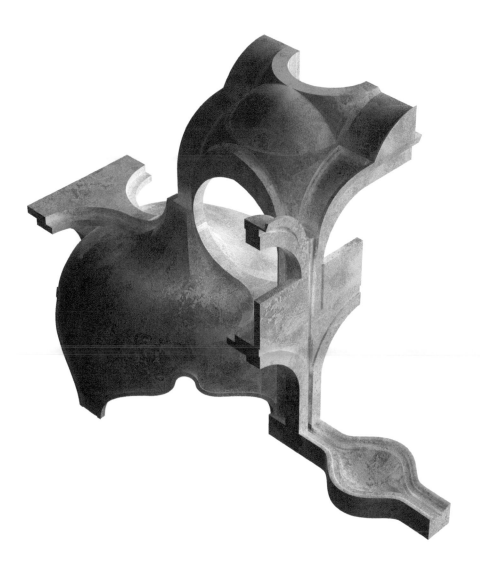

Figs. 2.12, 2.13

Figs. 2.14, 2.15

Figs. 2.16, 2.17

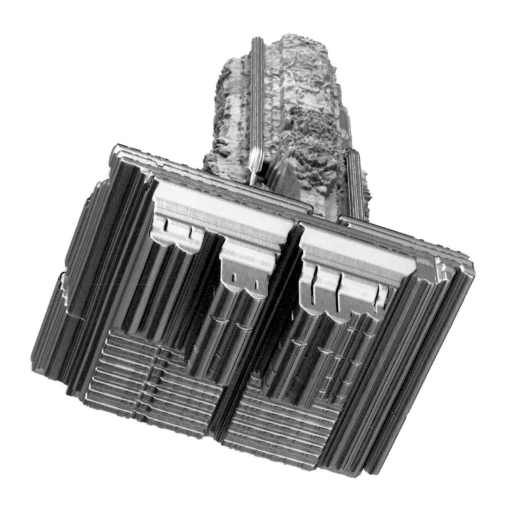

Figs. 2.18, 2.19

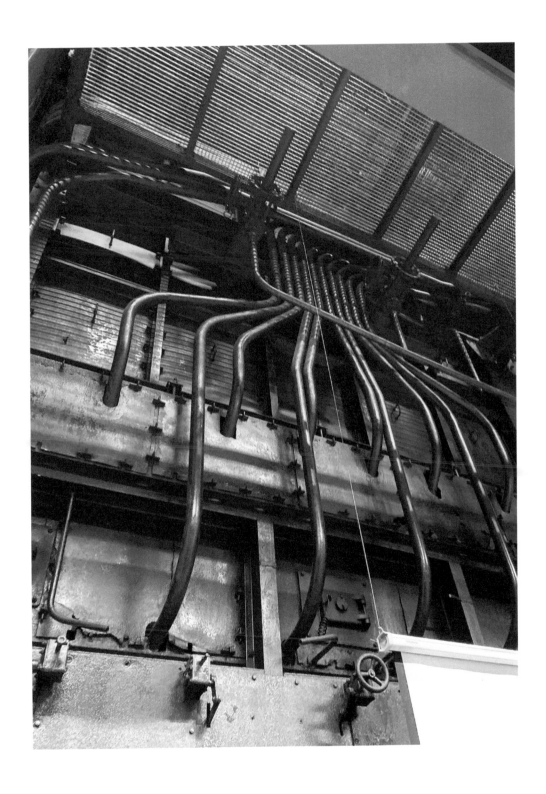

Figs. 2.20, 2.21

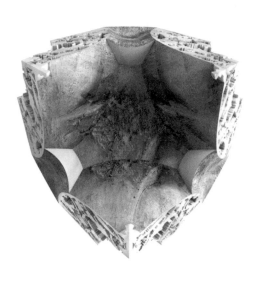

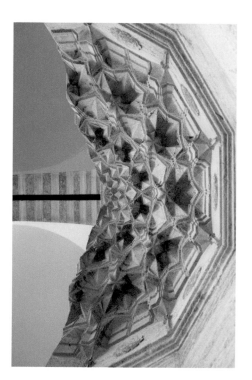

Figs. 2.22, 2.23

Figs. 2.24, 2.25

Istanbul

Figs. 2.26, 2.27

64

CAPTIONS

Fig. 2.2 Andrew Homick, Hybrid Artifact, rendering, Istanbul Studio, University of Pennsylvania Weitzman School of Design, 2018.

This artifact builds on the curved geometries of arches and domes. Its surface textures and figurations evoke Byzantine colors, themes, and iconography. The artifact seeks to capture both the historical qualities of Istanbul's ancient architecture and the abrupt juxtapositions in which they are often experienced today.

Fig. 2.3 Eminönü Istanbul, 2018. (Photograph courtesy Jennifer Minjee Son.)

An abrupt juxtaposition in Istanbul's Eminönü district. Arches, pendentives, and other remainders once belonging to a domed building are cut off by the exterior wall of a more recent residential one. The unlikely affinities between different ages, geometrical shapes, and formal expressions are on full display here.

Fig. 2.4 Caleb Ehly & Joonsung Lee, Hybrid Artifact, rendering, Istanbul Studio, University of Pennsylvania Weitzman School of Design, 2019.

The contours of common components of Ottoman architecture are appropriated and manipulated to create this artifact. Floral tiling, a typical motif in Islamic and Ottoman design, covers the whole object, giving it a quality of oscillation between figuration and abstraction.

Fig. 2.5 Süleymaniye Mosque, Istanbul, 2018. (Photograph courtesy Ryan Henriksen.)

To support the asymmetrical arches on each side, this unusual column in the courtyard of the famous Süleymaniye Mosque in Istanbul sports not one but two capitals stacked on top of each other and facing different directions. The slicing of the muqarnas provides an unexpected view into the capital's profile, and the off-balance transition between arches and column is further accentuated by two iron rods that reinforce the structure of the arches at different heights.

Fig. 2.6 Zehua Zhang, Hybrid Artifact, rendering, Istanbul Studio, University of Pennsylvania Weitzman School of Design, 2018.

This artifact reconfigures the intricate relationships between the shapes, geometries, and decorative motifs found in Ottoman mosques into a new hybridized form. Decontextualized and free from concerns of scale or structural necessity, the artifact explores ribbing as an expressive tool.

Fig. 2.7 Küçük Ayasofya Mosque (Church of Saints Sergius and Bacchus), Istanbul, 2018. (Photograph courtesy Ferda Kolatan.)

These intricately carved capitals and lintels hail back to the early Byzantine times when the church was first erected (between 527 and 536 CE). After Constantinople's conquest by the Ottoman Turks, the church was converted into a mosque and the original mosaics depicting Christian iconography were replaced by abstract patterns and calligraphical symbols. The alterations made to the Küçük Ayasofya's interior are a vivid example of an architecture that is expressed in contradictions.

Fig. 2.8 Nuruosmaniye Mosque Istanbul, 2018. (Photograph courtesy Ferda Kolatan.)

Interior view of the domed courtyard entrance to the Nuruosmaniye Mosque in Cemberlitaş, Istanbul. This mosque is renowned for its unique blend of European baroque-style elements and Ottoman Mosque typology. The architectural and artistic features of both Christian and Islamic traditions come together to form a mismatched yet cohesive whole, resulting in a curious display of unlikely affinities. These affinities can be observed in the intricate stained-glass windows, the corner ornaments, and most notably in the muqarnas, where the typical abstract geometrical pattern has been replaced by a figurative ornamentation of acanthus leaves. Additionally, a structural reinforcement rod supporting a halogen fixture adds yet another misfit element to the composition.

Fig. 2.9 Zehua Zhang & Zhuoqing Cai, Hybrid Artifact, rendering, Istanbul Studio, University of Pennsylvania Weitzman School of Design, 2018.

This rendering depicts a light fixture that has absorbed a mixture of architectural and ornamental qualities common in baroque-era mosques. The typical practice of minimizing the visibility of such fixtures so as not to interfere with the overall aesthetic of the building is here reversed. The utilitarian components become cultural artifacts in their own right.

Fig. 2.10 Eminönü, Istanbul, 2018.
(Photograph courtesy Ira Kapaj.)

This photograph captures an odd connection between two courtyard aisles. A recent marble arch has been attached to the midpoint of an older masonry arch, creating an unusual intersection of the two structures. The newer smaller arch sits atop a column that awkwardly disrupts the space of the original arch, seemingly growing out of its keystone. While this misfit is surely a consequence of poor planning or oversight, the odd coupling of arches offers an intriguing example of unlikely affinities in which the same tectonic components (arches) assemble in a rather unexpected fashion.

Fig. 2.11 Jennifer Minjee Son & Jingwen Luo, Hybrid Artifact, rendering, Istanbul Studio, University of Pennsylvania Weitzman School of Design, 2019.

This model explores the different formal, structural, and spatial qualities that can arise from a recombination of architectural components like arches, domes, and semi-domes. The customary orders of assembly are disregarded, allowing for atypical conditions to emerge.

Fig. 2.12 Topkapı Palace,Istanbul, 2018.
(Photograph courtesy Jennifer Minjee Son.)

A building in which various contradictory corner and entablature details constitute layers of a new form. Belonging to the historical Topkapı Palace in Istanbul, this detail is a consequence of the negotiation and resolution of the difference between component and floor heights. Remarkable is the attention given to the careful adornment of the stone profiles despite the overall incongruity of the corner elements.

Fig. 2.13 Caleb Ehly & Joonsung Lee, Hybrid Artifact, rendering, Istanbul Studio, University of Pennsylvania Weitzman School of Design, 2019.

Many corner details of older building stock in Istanbul incorporate various odd transitions. In some cases, these transitions are the result of changes to the building over time; in others, they reflect an accommodation of unorthodox interior and exterior conditions. This artifact combines a series of different corner details to form a new hybrid composition.

Fig. 2.14 Yuanyi Zhou & Wenjia Go, Hybrid Artifact, rendering, Istanbul Studio, University of Pennsylvania Weitzman School of Design, 2018.

This hybrid plays with our often predetermined assessments of value based on material and cultural features. A brass sprinkler head is merged with an upside-down Ottoman pavilion, estranging both forms and allowing for new readings and value assessments to take place. The combination of a uniform materiality and the illegibility of scale, purpose, or function evokes a sense of preciousness in this object.

Fig. 2.15 The roof structure of the Imperial Council building in Topkapı Palace,Istanbul, 2019. (Photograph courtesy Ferda Kolatan.)

The rich interplay between the gilded ornamentation, the marble column, and the security cameras and loudspeakers exposes unlikely affinities. Architectural themes from East and West (muqarnas-adorned capital and painted baroque cartouche), the mundane, ornamental, and technological all mingle into a cohesive whole.

Fig. 2.16 Dolmabahçe Palace, Istanbul, 2019. (Photograph courtesy Ferda Kolatan.)

The eclectic ornamentation on this fountain in the Dolmabahçe Palace is a common sight in Istanbul and reflects a broader trend in the city's architecture. Here, the mixture of stylistic and typological features from Western and Eastern traditions reaches back at least to the conversion of the Hagia Sophia into a mosque shortly after the city was taken by the Ottomans in 1453. However, this mixture of stylistic features across cultural and religious divides reached its apex in the 18th and 19th centuries. The fountain showcases the hybridization of European motifs like the C-scroll and acanthus leaf with floral compositions typical in Iznik tiling. Even the fountain itself is a hybridization of the rococo-inspired wall piece and a separate stone-cut water bowl.

Fig. 2.17 Emily Sun, Hybrid Artifact, rendering, Istanbul Studio, University of Pennsylvania Weitzman School of Design, 2019.

This rendering depicts a fountain designed using digital techniques derived from the traditional Turkish art form of ebru. The flowing patterns that come from painting on water are fused with the ornamental elements of the fountain to create an artifact that mirrors and estranges the many rococo-inspired fountains in Istanbul.

Fig. 2.18 Caleb Ehly & Joonsung Lee, Hybrid Artifact, rendering, Istanbul Studio, University of Pennsylvania Weitzman School of Design, 2019.

This artifact explores a hybrid aesthetic in which the material effects of industrial equipment combine with those of deteriorating concrete or other similar building materials. The base of the artifact is created by compressing polished metal piping into a solid "golden" mass, invoking contrasts with the rough and weathered surface of the wall fragment that sits atop it. The wall fragment has been cut and surface treated to create a unique visual effect evocative of a kind of alien monolith.

Fig. 2.19 Bilgi University, Istanbul, 2019. (Photograph courtesy Jennifer Minjee Son.)

Details from a dysfunctional boiler house take on new significance in the context of Bilgi University's campus architecture. Throughout Istanbul, but particularly along the Golden Horn, a large variety of decaying industrial sites are being adapted for contemporary reuse.

Fig. 2.20 Haliç Shipyard (formerly known as the Imperial Shipyard or Tersâne-i Âmire), Istanbul, 2019. (Photograph courtesy Andrew Homick.)

The shipyard belongs to a group of deteriorating industrial sites along the Golden Horn that are slated to be replaced with new mixed-use commercial developments. Around the drydocks, unlikely affinities have emerged between the colored mechanical pipes, the stained-stone steps of the basin, and the wooden planks used to stabilize the ships.

Fig. 2.21 Zoe Cennami & Margarida Mota, Hybrid Artifact, rendering, Istanbul Studio, University of Pennsylvania Weitzman School of Design, 2019.

The estranging effects of the weathering and corrosion of architectural materials are particularly perceptible in industrial sites. The aesthetic qualities that emerge from the natural processes of weathering and the synthetic processes of corrosion are intermixed and mapped onto a concrete component, which appears to be a fragment once belonging to a larger assembly.

Fig. 2.22 Jennifer Minjee Son & Jingwen Luo, Hybrid Artifact, rendering, Istanbul Studio, University of Pennsylvania Weitzman School of Design, 2019.

This artifact conjures a roof-like shape from an array of half and quarter domes. The section through the domes reveals a structure thickly ornamented with patterns reminiscent of the stone carvings in Islamic architecture. The lacy and delicate nature of these carvings contrasts with the domes but is also inseparable from them.

Fig. 2.23 Süleymaniye Mosque, Istanbul, 2019. (Photograph courtesy Ferda Kolatan.)

A wall niche in the Süleymaniye courtyard shows how the muqarnas is utilized to fuse wall and ceiling elements together. Visible from the front (elevation) and from underneath (reflected ceiling plan), the muqarnas is a unique transitional ornament that affects our experience of space and our understanding of tectonic components.

Fig. 2.24 Istanbul, 2019. (Photograph courtesy Joonsung Lee.)

Marble is a ubiquitous material in Istanbul, used in ancient and contemporary buildings to convey both luxury and utility. The photograph depicts a curious ensemble of marble elements without distinction between the practical and the ornamental. Two unremarkable blocks stacked on top of each other serve as a terracing device for water spilling out of a small opening in the wall behind them. A shortened pilaster provides support for a half column resting on top of it, while gold-painted details add an unexpected touch of luxury to an otherwise random-seeming grouping of components. The marble's once straight edges have rounded over time, giving the odd assembly a rather soft and organic feel.

Fig. 2.25 Caleb Ehly & Joonsung Lee, Hybrid Artifact, rendering, Istanbul Studio, University of Pennsylvania Weitzman School of Design, 2019.

Relief-like details carved into stone lintels are extrapolated into a three-dimensional object. An array of existing and partially reconfigured mechanical parts, commonly used in the hallways of Istanbul apartment buildings, have been assembled into a hybrid concoction of tubes that hang from the object like stalactites. The boundary between practical and decorative elements dissolves as they intermingle and merge within intricate concatenations.

Fig. 2.26 Tophane Fountain, Istanbul, 2019. (Photograph courtesy Ferda Kolatan.)

The Tophane Fountain, built in 1732, features exquisite rococo elements as well as intricate muqarnas and floral motifs. It is widely recognized as one of Istanbul's most famous and revered public fountains.

Fig. 2.27 Yuanyi Zhou & Wenjia Go, Hybrid Artifact, rendering, Istanbul Studio, University of Pennsylvania Weitzman School of Design, 2018.

The model depicts a partial section of a park situated on a hillside diagonally across from the Tophane Fountain. The fountain's decorative elements are skillfully integrated into the concrete retaining walls and terraces, creating an unexpected dialogue with the carvings of the excavator machine, which are left visible along the walking path. To further enhance the interplay between nature and culture, the flowing colors running down the walls and terraces match the hues of the surrounding plants.

Ambiguous Architecture

Tophane, Istanbul

Wandering through the neighborhoods of Istanbul is a captivating experience. At every turn, attractions of some kind await: magnificent buildings spanning centuries, steep hills opening to sweeping vistas, and the unceasing vitality of its busy streets, which have borne witness to a plethora of cultural and commercial practices, everyday customs, and countless other miscellaneous human interactions that have shaped the city over millennia. The hallmark of any great city is usually considered its iconic landmarks–the historical edifices that pay tribute to a storied past and punctuate the city with memorable sights that ignite the imagination of locals and visitors alike. Istanbul, the capital of past empires nestled along the sublime coasts of the Golden Horn and the Bosphorus Strait, has many such landmarks, ranging from ornate street fountains to ancient ruins and awe-inspiring mosques.

What is often overlooked in lofty determinations of a city's greatness, however, is the critical role played by the gradual accumulation of vastly disparate architectural elements that subtly shape the very fabric from which all urban forms and activities ultimately derive. These elements encompass the ordinary as well as the extraordinary, the artifactual and the infrastructural, the complete, fragmented, and the residual. These accumulations are often the results of attempts to connect, modify, or mend structures, obfuscating the boundaries of their identities. In other instances, their components have simply fallen out of sync with one another; and, in yet others, they describe situations where material and cultural practices intersect unexpectedly. While these architectural formations are integral to the social, aesthetic, and cultural life of the city, they often go unrecognized due to their ambiguous nature.

This ambiguous architecture exists in stark contrast to the buildings we promptly recognize as culturally or historically significant. The reduction of a city's architecture to these select structures or sites, whether consciously or not, is all too common. Often conveyed through unambiguous postcard-like representations, these buildings and locations attain their iconic status by being easily identifiable. This renowned architecture provides a convenient means of branding cities, showcasing their highlights, and, in turn, concealing their perceived shortcomings. The vast majority of urban elements and their interactions, particularly the kind of

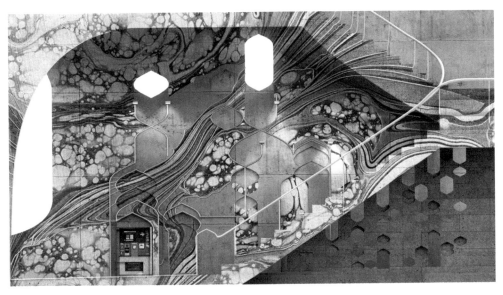

Fig. 2.28 Carla Bonilla & Yang Li & Neera Sharma, Tophane, rendering, Istanbul Studio, University of Pennsylvania Weitzman School of Design, 2018.

objects and object relations that are harder to grasp with clarity, become thus more prone to being disregarded as *meaningless*.

But meaning often arises from improbable or bewildering circumstances. Ambiguity can be thus understood as a destabilizing feature that renders an object intriguing, prompting us to discover or define said object in novel or unprecedented ways. For the literary critic William Empson, *ambiguity* has a series of possible meanings and represents a crucial aesthetic element of literature: "'Ambiguity' itself can mean an indecision as to what you mean, an intention to mean several things, a probability that one or other or both of two things has been meant, and the fact that a statement has several meanings."[52]

The relevance of ambiguity to hybrid design–in its embrace of multiple meanings and its resistance to singular interpretations–should, by now, be evident to the reader. It is worth noting, however, that the aforementioned landmarks and iconic buildings are often just as ambiguous as their more mundane and misfit counterparts. Riddled with contradictions and oddities, they are far from the monolithic commemorations of singular historical events–frozen in time, unyielding in their authority, and unaffected by the haphazard and accidental processes that shape the rest of the city–that their postcard images would suggest. To the contrary, many of these landmarks are, in fact, equally impacted by material, stylistic, and programmatic entanglements. The distinction lies in the common assumption that what makes landmarks meaningful is their cohesiveness, purity, and integrity as a kind of total architecture–a perception that is perpetuated by the proliferation of standardized reproductions across print and digital media. Naturally, these depictions tend to exclude any underlying tensions, deviations, or discontinuities that may upon closer examination characterize the landmark more accurately, adding to its overall complexity and appeal.[53]

To acknowledge that all buildings, to at least some degree, draw meaning or significance from their ambiguous qualities prompts a reassessment of how we think of purpose, meaning, or value in architecture. These ambiguous qualities can be considered as productive, meaningful, and valuable in and of themselves, irrespective of the status of their host buildings. In this case, the categorical distinctions according to which some buildings are classified as landmarks, others as ordinary, and still others as not architecture at all would no longer be the sole determinant of architecture's worth. Other commonly neglected factors would come to the fore, crossovers between different categories would become possible, and the opportunities to explore new avenues for design would grow exponentially.

Fig. 2.29 Carla Bonilla & Yang Li & Neera Sharma, Tophane, rendered photomontage, Istanbul Studio, University of Pennsylvania Weitzman School of Design, 2018.

The tram station (foreground) draws unlikely affinities to the historic Tophane foundry behind it. A mural evoking ebru, the traditional Turkish art of paper marbling, fuses with the architectural details of the concrete canopy, pedestrian bridge, and surrounding street infrastructure. (See also: Fig. 1.13.)

Fig. 2.30 Yibo Ma, Bleachers, rendered photomontage, Istanbul Studio, University of Pennsylvania Weitzman School of Design, 2018.

Site: Tophane

A series of loosely connected sites and buildings in Istanbul's Tophane district are here repurposed in new roles after the neighborhood's expansion has left them in a state of disarray and ambiguity.[54] The first project involves the redesign of the existing Tophane tram station. Various components commonly found in tram and subway stations, such as handrails, wiring, lighting fixtures, or vending machines, undergo subtle alterations and reconfigurations in their relationships to one another (**Fig. 2.28**). The shapes and profiles of buildings in the station's vicinity, along with recognizable graphic and artistic motifs, are integrated in a strangely familiar image representing the tram station and its immediate surroundings as a blend of different objects. As one approaches the station from a distance, its material affinities with the historic Tophane building situated right behind it become apparent (**Figs. 2.29, 1.13**). Color palettes reveal unexpected kinships between these otherwise rather distinct building types, as does the interplay between rectangular and curvilinear architectural components.

Just a couple of blocks down from the Tophane foundry, along the same tram line, one encounters a small outdoor recreation facility. Surrounded by busy streets and immersed in a vibrant local scene, this unassuming sports field remains inconspicuous due to its slightly elevated position above street level. Once inside, however, players and visitors are rewarded with unexpected views of the exquisite 16th-century Kılıç Ali Paşa Mosque.[55] The standard fencing that surrounds the compact field is lightly modified and woven into the metal structure of the bleachers

(Fig. 2.30). Functional elements seamlessly transform into ornamental features, producing architectural effects on an intimate scale, utilizing only locally sourced materials. Freestanding streetlights that illuminate the field are also integrated into the fence, creating a cohesive ensemble of objects with the bleachers. By encircling the sports facility, the fence not only prevents balls and other equipment from falling onto the street but also provides the open court with urban definition and architectural autonomy.

On the other side of the Tophane armory is the Sanatkarlar Park. This narrow and elongated public green space sits on the side of a steep hill, providing views of both the street with the tram line and the Bosphorus strait beyond. Ambling

Fig. 2.31 Yuanyi Zhou & Wenjia Go, Sanatkarlar Park, rendered photomontage, Istanbul Studio, University of Pennsylvania Weitzman School of Design, 2018.

Next to the Tophane foundry, Sanatkarlar Park offers sweeping views of the Bosphorus. However, it's difficult to access due to its location on a steep hill. To address this difficulty, the concrete retaining walls and terraces are incorporated to stabilize the hillside for visitors. The design seamlessly integrates traces left by terraforming machines with the ornamented concrete walls. These walls feature geometries reminiscent of muqarnas, adding a layer of estrangement to these traditional forms.

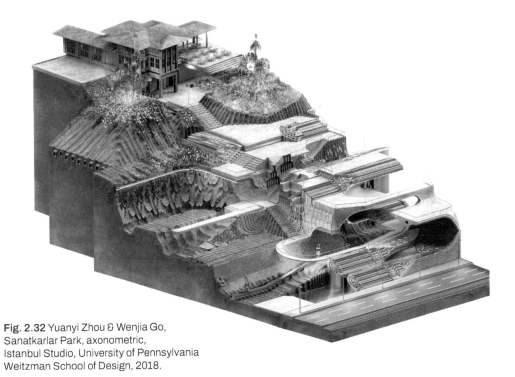

Fig. 2.32 Yuanyi Zhou & Wenjia Go,
Sanatkarlar Park, axonometric,
Istanbul Studio, University of Pennsylvania
Weitzman School of Design, 2018.

along its meandering pathways, one encounters a series of terraces connecting
the hilltop, which is occupied by a tea house, to the street level below (**Figs. 2.31,
2.32**). These terraces incorporate the concrete retaining walls, creating a uniquely
hybrid ground that defies straightforward typological definitions such as park,
building, or infrastructure. The scars and traces left by the machines involved in
the terraforming process, along with the intentionally designed grooves and ridges
within the concrete formwork, become an important aspect of the park's aesthetic
(**Fig. 2.35**). The resulting patterns are partially colored and evoke the formal
intricacy of the *muqarnas*, a popular form of ornament in traditional Islamic architecture.[56] Additionally, water lines used for plant irrigation are creatively bent into
sculptural scaffolds, supporting vegetation and contributing to the formation of
further hybrid artifacts within the park (**Figs. 2.33, 2.34**).

Occasionally, smaller hybrid artifacts in the form of public fountains adorn the
rough surfaces of the many walls that line the hilly streets of the Tophane neighborhood (**Fig. 2.36**).[57] Here again, the designs primarily utilize materials, colors, and
objects that are both familiar and available locally. These items, often sourced from
hardware stores, are incorporated into existing building components to create ad
hoc and small-scale architectural interventions that enliven the streets by inviting
inhabitants to engage with their city in a more direct and spontaneous fashion.

Fig. 2.33, 2.34 Yuanyi Zhou & Wenjia Go, Irrigation Artifacts, renderings, Istanbul Studio, University of Pennsylvania Weitzman School of Design, 2018.

Fig. 2.35 Yuanyi Zhou & Wenjia Go, Sanatkarlar Park, rendered photomontage, Istanbul Studio, University of Pennsylvania Weitzman School of Design, 2018.

The terraces and retaining walls of Sanatkarlar Park form a meandering path that leads up the hill. The design incorporates cultural features that aesthetically align with the traces left by the construction machines and materials used to build the park. This unique combination of elements gives rise to a new architecture, showcasing a curious blend of diverse influences.

NOTES

52   William Empson, *Seven Types of Ambiguity* (New York: New Directions Publishing, 1947), 5.

53   The universally acclaimed Hagia Sophia is a prime example of this phenomenon. Built between 532 and 537 CE during the reign of Byzantine emperor Justinian, this famous basilica exhibited hybrid qualities from its inception. The pairing of a circular dome with an elongated nave combined Latin and Byzantine styles. Some of its decorative elements, such as impost capitals, cornices, and marble revetments, were idiosyncratic enough to prompt European visitors in previous centuries to view the edifice as "eccentric and degenerate." See Cyril Mango, *Hagia Sophia, A Vision for Empires* (Istanbul: Ertuğ & Kocabıyık, 1997), XXXIX. Following the conquest of Constantinople by the Ottoman Turks in 1453, the church was converted into a mosque. Most of its Christian icons and mosaics were either destroyed, covered up, or replaced by Islamic patterns and geometric wood carvings. Four minarets, a mihrab, and a minbar were added to complete the conversion, accompanied by numerous other changes, repairs, and reinforcements over the subsequent centuries. In the 19th and early 20th centuries, as Ottoman rulers became more receptive to Western influences, efforts to uncover and restore the lost Byzantine mosaics commenced. Ultimately, the Hagia Sophia was converted into a museum during the early years of the Turkish Republic, only to be reconverted into a mosque in 2020. Despite the diverse and sometimes contradictory influences on its architecture, the Hagia Sophia is typically depicted as a cohesive and total artifact, evident in the limited representational views presented repeatedly on postcards, web images, and other reproductive media.

54   The Tophane district developed around the historic Ottoman cannon foundry (Tophane-i Amire), originally built by Sultan Mehmet II during the 15th century and subsequently rebuilt numerous times due to fires and renovations. The labyrinthine neighborhood expands up the hill north of the Tophane and is abruptly cut off at the bottom by a multilane vehicular road, which also incorporates a tramway line and station. Across from the tram station lies the new Galataport ferry terminal with its adjacent restaurants and high-end shopping malls. Squeezed in between are several other historically noteworthy buildings, including the Kılıç Ali Paşa and Nusretiye mosques and the Tophane Fountain. The convergence of all these diverse urban elements makes the Tophane district particularly interesting for exploring misfit conditions.

55   The Kılıç Ali Paşa mosque was built by Mimar Sinan in the 1580s. Sinan is widely recognized as the leading architect of the classical Ottoman period during the reign of Sultan Süleyman "the Magnificent." Sinan built hundreds of structures, most famously the Seliminiye mosque in Edirne and the Süleymaniye in Istanbul.

56   The muqarnas, a common Islamic ornament, is used to cover vaults, domes, niches, and column capitals in intricate three-dimensional patterns. Typically carved from stone or plaster, the muqarnas is based on complex geometrical structures reminiscent of stalactites or honeycombs and is often adorned with vibrant hues or calligraphic symbols. See Figs. 2.23 and 2.26.

57   Public fountains were widely used during the Ottoman Empire for both religious and hygienic reasons. Even today, almost every street in Istanbul has a functioning fountain or water spigot, often installed on the surface of a building facade or a retaining wall.

Fig. 2.36 Chae Young Kim & Haeyun Kwon, Fountains, rendering, Istanbul Studio, University of Pennsylvania Weitzman School of Design, 2018.

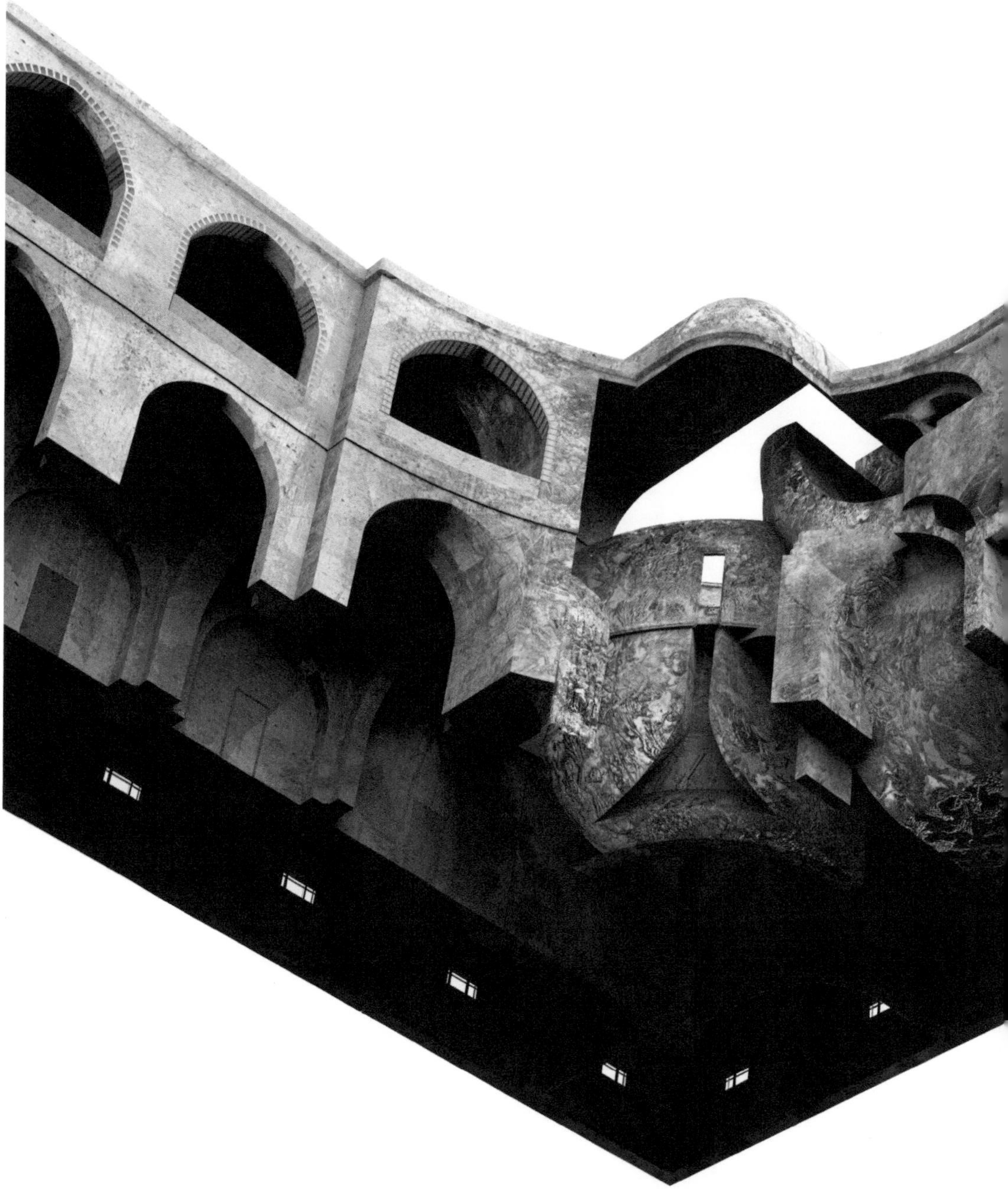

Fig. 2.37 Ira Kapaj & Kimberly Shoemaker
Büyük Valide Han, Istanbul, rendering.
Istanbul Studio, University of Pennsylvania
Weitzman School of Design, 2019.

Withdrawn Landmark

Büyük Valide Han, Istanbul

Istanbul is home to a wealth of architecture that, despite having once played a significant role in the cultural fabric of the city, is now forgotten. With the passage of time and the relentless push toward modernization, most buildings have a predictable life cycle: a slow decay, followed by a loss of functionality and eventual demolition; that is, unless they are deemed historically valuable. Only then are they likely to be preserved or even legally protected as landmarks. Landmarking, however, comes with its own rules, restrictions, and regulations, all of which serve the objective to restore a building to its assumed original condition and maintain it that way for posterity.

In some cases, particularly in Istanbul, buildings of significant historical value are so deeply ingrained within the city's fast-moving material and programmatic activities that a more dynamic alternative to traditional modes of preservation becomes not only desirable but necessary. Such an alternative would explore more targeted upgrades that are invested in the building's original typology, features, and characteristics, while also taking into account the need to re-engage with the urban flow and cultural context that is the lifeblood of the contemporary city. The Büyük Valide Han, built in the 17th century, is one such case and exemplifies the potential of an alternative approach to preserving historical buildings.

The Han sits at the heart of an industrious commercial district filled with small shops. Over centuries, it has endured fires, earthquakes, and countless modifications, all of which have left their indelible marks on it. The city has grown densely around the Han, almost absorbing the old structure entirely and rendering it barely visible. Consequently, the shopkeepers and artisans that occupied the building have been slowly forced out, unable to compete with the fast-paced world outside. Despite being placed under landmark protection in 1983, the authorities have made no efforts to repair or maintain the Han to date, ensuring its ongoing decline. As it stands, this unique building has little value for either the inhabitants of the neighborhood or the throngs of tourists who pass by daily without noticing it.

The projects in this section aim to repurpose and revitalize the Han by seizing on its peculiar predicament as a sanctuary of sorts, a withdrawn landmark involuntarily fortified by the densification of the city. The countless ad hoc alterations to the structure over time are, in these projects, understood as significant in their own right. These changes, while largely illegal and in violation of the landmark

Fig. 2.38 Büyük Valide Han, Istanbul, rendering.
Istanbul Studio, University of Pennsylvania Weitzman School of Design, 2019.

A **han** is an urban variant of the caravanserai, which emerged as a type of fortified trading post in Persia and the Middle East during the early era of regional trading routes (Silk Road). While, used primarily as a market, the *caravanserai* was also a place where traveling merchants could rest, eat, pray, and gossip amongst themselves. As such, the caravanserai can be understood as a sort of social and cultural hub where ideas were exchanged as much as goods.

During the period of the Seljuk Turks (from 1000 to 1300 AD), a vast network of these trading posts connected most of Asia Minor and modern-day Turkey. The popularity of hans continued throughout the centuries of Ottoman rule, with one of its most famous examples being the Grand Bazaar in Istanbul. Before sprawling into its current size over centuries of unmitigated growth, the Grand Bazaar was originally constructed shortly after the conquest of Constantinople as a modestly sized market. While some hans in Istanbul, like the Grand Bazaar or the Spice Bazaar (or Egyptian Bazaar), continue to attract visitors and prosper, many of the smaller ones have been forgotten in the modern period. The rigid center-oriented layout of the han typology is no match for the street-facing storefronts or large department stores that have become the norm today. While the han as a commercial type

is disappearing, many of the local commercial habits of today are still rooted in the customs and politics first cultured in these ancient trading posts. Haggling and bargaining, for instance, are still common practices when shopping in more traditional places in Istanbul, as is the obligatory offering of tea and brief conversation, which are viewed as prerequisites for good salesmanship.

The architecture of the han usually accommodates a one- or two-story building and follows a clear organizational principle. Originating from the roadside caravanserai and its need to protect its vendors and their merchandise from unwanted intruders, the building is laid out as an enclosed fort with a main gate that could be easily guarded. Individual stalls typically line all four sides of the square or rectangular plan and would serve as shops, lodgings, guestrooms, storage, and stables. The large central courtyard provided an open-air gathering area, additional space for trading and, in some cases, contained a small mosque for worship. Many urban hans have maintained the overall features of the caravanserai but have taken on odd shapes as they expand into neighboring areas.

code, nonetheless speak to the powerful efforts of the Han's occupants to maintain a minimum of functionality and prolong its life against all odds. Through these spontaneous alterations, architecture reveals a capacity to draw unexpected participation from its users, generating creative forms of maintenance and a plethora of misfit opportunities for hybrid design.

Site: The Hidden Han

The Büyük Valide Han is tucked away in Istanbul's busy Eminönü district, along the way between the Egyptian Spice Market and the Grand Bazaar. For those unfamiliar with the neighborhood, the Büyük Valide Han might as well not exist. Its main entrance is almost impossible to find, obscured by rows of colorful storefronts that have wedged into its many nooks and crannies, covering most of its outer walls with merchandise like clothing and cookware. From the bustling streets outside, one would hardly know that a building of considerable size, geometrical clarity, and cultural significance lies within.

Once inside, however, the atmosphere shifts dramatically. The noises, colors, and textures dominating the new "envelope" suddenly give way to an unexpected, almost serene calmness prevailing in the dimly lit aisles of the Han. Despite plaster repairs, faux ceilings, iron support rods, electrical cables, and junction boxes covering much of the original brick vaulting structure, the Han holds a mysterious beauty. The top portions of the transverse ribs that stretch across the bays are still intact, and as they extend in a steady sequence of arched thresholds they create a disorienting effect, much like being inside a hall of mirrors.

The Han's two floors are connected by stairs–some of which were added later and are made of concrete or metal–that lead to a hidden mezzanine that once housed the storage rooms for the dozens of shops that lined the courtyard. While the upper floor allows for occasional glimpses into the open courtyard, most of the exterior arches have been closed up haphazardly, creating long, dark, and claustrophobic tunnels. A narrow corner stair, hidden and off-limits to visitors, leads to the roof where unexpectedly wide views over the Han complex and its surroundings emerge, offering spectacular vistas that stretch as far as the Bosphorus and the Asian side of the city. Down below, however, the partly overgrown and partly overbuilt remains of the Han and its courtyard offer a stark contrast.

The abrupt atmospheric and spatial transitions one experiences when stepping across the multiple horizontal and vertical thresholds of the Han are a result of the building's gradual decay and its increasing seclusion from the active street life, but these new qualities are evident to anyone who does happen to stumble upon the site. In the not-so-distant past, the lively commotion from outside would flow uninterruptedly into the courtyard and from there farther into the Han's interior.

Figs. 2.39, 2.40, 2.41 Büyük Validiye Han, Istanbul, 2021. (Photograph courtesy Ferda Kolatan.)

The **Büyük Valide Han** is the largest bazaar in Istanbul built according to the traditional caravanserai typology. It was commissioned in 1651 by Kösem Valide Sultan—the mother of two sultans, Murat IV and Ibrahim, making her one of the most powerful and influential women of the Ottoman era. The Han is organized around a central rectangular courtyard measuring roughly 66 by 63 meters. Two smaller courtyards, one on the northern side of the main courtyard and the other on its southern side, were later added to the structure. The smallest, southern courtyard has a wedge-like triangular shape to accommodate the street and row of houses that run diagonally in front of the Han's main entrance gate. The northern rectangular courtyard was built around the remains of an old Byzantine tower (Tower of Eirene) in the northeastern corner of the complex. The upper portion of the masonry tower was partly destroyed, most likely by an earthquake.

During the 19th century, the Han was predominantly used by Iranian merchants who had formed a large community in the area since the days of the Silk Road. Located at the center of the large courtyard is a Shi'a Mosque, rebuilt multiple times and still in use today. In total, the Büyük Valide Han comprises 210 similarly sized cells across two floors that once housed a mixture of different vendors, artisans, craftsmen, printmakers, and innkeepers. Many of the rooms were used as ateliers for metal and textile crafts, the products of which were sold in adjacent shops.

The decline of the Han began in the early 20th century, and by the 1970s it was mostly used as a storage depot. In 1983 the complex was declared a protected landmark and has since been left untouched without any efforts to halt its decay. Today, a few vendors and craftspeople remain in the building, but most of it is vacant or still used for storage. When the Büyük Valide Han was built, the main entrance (Fig. 2.39) was easily discernible from the street. As the city grew denser over time, the Han receded into the surrounding urban fabric, obscuring its presence and giving it a withdrawn character. The arched hallways of the Han (Fig. 2.40) were once open to the courtyard and filled with light. The barricading of many arches to create more enclosed space created the dark and inhospitable corridors we see today. From inside the courtyard (Fig. 2.41), the ad hoc attempts to create interior space take on odd and haphazard forms. Arches have been filled in, and doors, windows, stairs, and other components have been added in an irregular fashion.

Today, these same spaces offer a sanctuary amidst the raucous street activities, imbuing the Han with an almost monastery-like atmosphere.

In addition to this quality of seclusion is the dizzying array of alterations made by the Han's occupants over time in efforts to maintain the structure. Such efforts are visible all over the vaults, arches, walls, ceilings, stairs, and floors of the old building. Rusty signs advertising shops long gone; haphazard attempts at repair and beautification; added alcoves arrhythmically poking into the courtyard; and indiscriminately placed electrical wires, telephone cables, plumbing pipes, and satellite dishes hang on to the Han's masonry like strange adornments from a promised future that never fully arrived.

The projects in this section acknowledge the Han as a historical treasure but do not equate its authenticity with an original state. Instead, they focus on the present and explore its myriad misfit conditions for what they are and for what they could yield in the future. In the past, the Büyük Valide Han was renowned for its shops, inns, and local artisans who would attract a steady stream of customers from far and wide. Tea-drinking locals hunched over backgammon boards, curious groupings of haggling merchants and their customers, and the occasional traveler driven here in hopes of discovery and adventure would all mix in the courtyard and under the shady archways.

Today, such an image might seem quaint, evoking a nostalgia for days of yore rather than possible futures. To try and elevate the building through the traditional means of historical preservation seems especially pointless as the Han cannot be freed up and laid bare as it once was without demolishing large portions of the surrounding building stock and severely undermining the neighborhood's economic and cultural identity. It is in this spirit that the following projects take up the problem of the Büyük Valide Han, imagining hybrid architectures that align with its current spatial and aesthetic conditions and derive new functional and programmatic purposes from them.

Each of the following four projects takes a unique approach the problem of the Han. Altered Arches closely examines existing building structures and details in order to derive subtle variations from them. Mundane additions to the Han and quotidian objects strewn about are considered with the same carefulness as the main architecture and are integrated in a series of artifacts that guide the visitor through the building. The Nested Pavilion focuses on the Han's peculiar interlocking between courtyards and building components. It derives an intricate scheme of voids and masses that utilize the many misalignments that have transformed the complex over time. The Performing Han revives the traditional craft and artisan ateliers and choreographs their activities into a larger theatrical production, highlighting the collaborative and aesthetic performances of machines, materials, and architecture. And finally, The Bird Sanctuary seizes on the great number of migratory birds that congregate around the Han, converting the building's facades and main courtyard into an aviary where human and nonhuman interests coexist.

Altered Arches

Altered Arches aims to free up the dark barricaded hallways of the Han and turn them into accessible and usable spaces while maintaining the building's misfit character and incorporating its many aberrations into a unique design proposal. This is achieved through a number of episodic interventions to the arches, vaults, domes, and stairs of the Han, which are tweaked and carefully amended without significantly changing the building's structure. The goal is to celebrate the Han not in its pure state as a tectonic or typological exemplar but as an aggregate form. The arches are explored in their capacity to generate multiple variations by organizing their components in unorthodox ways and adorning their surfaces with tiling and hardware commonly used inside the Han complex. Once linked together, these altered arches create new focal points within the Han and draw visitors to explore them from different angles.

Fig. 2.42 Ryan Henriksen & Tae Hyung, Altered Arches, renderings, Istanbul Studio, University of Pennsylvania Weitzman School of Design, 2019.

Figs. 2.43, 2.44 Above and opposite: Ryan Henriksen & Tae Hyung, Altered Arches, powder-print model, Istanbul Studio, University of Pennsylvania Weitzman School of Design, 2019.

One of the most prominent features of the Büyük Valide Han are the forty-nine vaults that line the arched aisles in a strict staccato framing the courtyard. Divided into two rows, the aisles were used by the shopkeepers and artisans to exhibit and store their goods. The outer aisle, facing the courtyard, served as a social and display area, whereas the inner aisle, facing the walls, provided semi-enclosed storage spaces for the shops. Today, with most of the stores gone, the two-story archways resemble a cloister more than they do a marketplace, tempting the visitor to walk inside the corridors and experience the continuity of empty, vacated spaces rather than the bustle of individual shops.

The uncovered upper portion of the arches and vaults creates a repetitive, almost classical rhythm that contrasts sharply with the lower parts that are mostly covered and retrofitted with a haphazard assembly of temporary walls, sheds, makeshift stairs, and other ad hoc structures and furnishings. On the second floor, the vaults

Figs. 2.45, 2.46 Above and opposite: Ryan Henriksen & Tae Hyung, Altered Arches, renderings, Istanbul Studio, University of Pennsylvania Weitzman School of Design, 2019.

With minimal intervention, the two floors of the Han are remodeled and made accessible to visitors. The closed-up and barricaded archways are opened on both sides to allow the flow of natural light back into the building. Tiled skylights are integrated into the domes, and fountains into their supporting piers. The incorporation of new elements does not significantly alter the original architecture but estranges it just enough to draw attention to its remarkable structure and odd detailing.

culminate in brick domes, many of which are heavily deteriorated and partly collapsed. The roof itself, where sweeping views across the neighborhood await, is accessible only illegally from a hidden corner of the Han. The artifacts in this project refashion the stairs and arches, strategically cutting and carving into the domes to facilitate an easier and more engaging passage through the Han and all the way to the roof.

While the effects of uncoordinated additions and decay can be viewed as detrimental to the Han's planimetric and organizational clarity, these elements do add a sense of suspense and unpredictability to its architecture. Altered Arches recognizes, and even cherishes, this fact, articulating a whimsical and fragmentary aesthetic to match it. Plumbing and electrical equipment, residual tiling, and other decorative bits and pieces are integrated into the newly repurposed hybrid arches in unorthodox ways.

Altered Arches proposes a unique approach to dealing with historical buildings by treating their individual parts as semiautonomous objects that can both preserve the historical features of a building and develop new iterations from their designs. The curious detailing of the arches and the fusion of ornament with functional and structural elements are entirely contingent on the material and cultural histories of the Han. And yet, by forging unexpected relationships, the arches and stairways

Fig. 2.47 Ryan Henriksen & Tae Hyung, Altered Arches, rendered photomontage, Istanbul Studio, University of Pennsylvania Weitzman School of Design, 2019.

Altered Arches picks up on an important characteristic feature of the Han in its current state. Ad hoc additions and alterations to the arches and vaults of the building are treated not as undesirable deviations from the original but as opportunities to develop a unique structural and formal language that reflects the current realities of the site. This language incorporates mundane components like tiling, handrails, and fountains into new hybrid forms.

challenge our perceptual routines and illustrate architecture's capacity for reinvention, not only as a polished landmark, but as a vital constitutive element for contemporary design.

The Nested Pavilion

The Nested Pavilion picks up on the spatial and material incongruencies of the Büyük Valide Han and employs them in the construction of a novel underground architecture that serves as a venue for cultural events. Cultural programs are sorely missing in this neighborhood, which becomes deserted in the afternoon and early evening once commercial activities cease. The project takes up the unusual nesting of architectural spaces and components at the main entrance of the Han–the results of the many misalignments and alterations the building has been subjected to over its long history. Following the tenets of misfit and hybrid architecture, the pavilion forges new collaborative and aesthetic relations rather than seeking to restore the architecture to an earlier state or to declutter it by minimizing the appearance of the interventions that have become its core characteristics.

Currently, the main entry to the Büyük Valide Han is located at the center of its southernmost facade, along a highly trafficked pedestrian shopping street. The only distinguishing mark of the entrance gate is a modest stone jutty above its archway. The rest of the exterior facade is an amorphous patchwork of individual storefronts.

Figs. 2.48, 2.49 Above and opposite: Caleb Ehly & Joonsung Lee, Nested Pavilion, renderings, Istanbul Studio, University of Pennsylvania Weitzman School of Design, 2019.

These renderings show the sequencing of the interstitial spaces from which the Nested Pavilion emerges. The main entrance of the Han leads to the triangular courtyard and from there into the negative volume below, which forms the main event space of the Pavilion. Behind it, additional spaces from the Han are appropriated to serve various functional needs and connect visitors to the building's other areas.

Figs. 2.50, 2.51 Caleb Ehly & Joonsung Lee, Nested Pavilion, renderings,
Istanbul Studio, University of Pennsylvania Weitzman School of Design, 2019.

These two renderings depict some of the Nested Pavilion's unique details and ornaments. Material residues and mismatched components are developed into new tectonic and surface expressions. A continuous metallic sheen is applied to evoke a sense of coherence and preciousness across the disparate elements.

A short corridor leads from the street to the first and smallest of the Han's three courtyards, which was originally shaped like a triangle, but numerous shack-like additions have since diffused any legible perimeter. From here, one enters into the main Han building through another dark hallway without much notice. The southern exterior facade of the Han doubles as the interior wall for the triangular courtyard, resulting in a curious nesting of masses and voids.

This unique sequencing of facades and courtyards, the play between interior and exterior, is the locus of the Nested Pavilion. The original triangular shape of the courtyard is extruded downward to form a negative volume. Portions of the Han are cut into and extracted to accommodate for auxiliary programs and new circulatory routes for the Pavilion. Two symmetrical stairways branch off on either side of the main entrance and connect the street level to the buried volume of the negative triangle. A series of adjacent interstitial spaces are created, expanding on the existing qualities of the site and incorporating them into a contemporary Piranesian architecture.

The Nested Pavilion is a formal and conceptual inversion of the commonly free-standing and easily approachable pavilion type. Rather than an object distinct from its environment, the pavilion is submerged into the deep, historical layers of the old Han and seamlessly integrated therein. The colors and patterns of the Pavilion are inspired by the tones, textures, and shades of the surrounding buildings, while the

Fig. 2.52 Detail Büyük Valide Han, Istanbul, 2019.(Photograph courtesy Caleb Ehly.)

The walls of the Büyük Valide Han evince its numerous alterations and additions. These markings embellish the building with intriguing details and unique component combinations.

metallic sheen adds a play on the dichotomy between the ordinary and the extraordinary, an important aspect of hybrid artifacts. Over time, the layering of different materials combined with weathering has created a smudgy patina that covers the hallways of the Han. The models show a fictitious, polished version that deliberately plays on the tension between the residue, often overlooked as commonplace, and the preciousness (and cost) associated with metallic material coatings.

The Performing Han

In its heyday, the Büyük Valide Han was occupied by hundreds of artisans and craftspeople who labored year round to produce goods for the city at large and contribute to the vitality of the local communities in and around the bazaar district. The shops in the Han were equipped with various tools and machines suited for small-scale, manual labor. But with the onset of industrialization, the occupants of the Han could no longer compete with the vendors along the more accessible streets outside. As a result, artisans and shop owners began to move out and relocate their businesses to more peripheral parts of the city. The Performing Han aims to revive the historical significance of the Büyük Valide Han as a manufacturing venue by showcasing its long-lost functions, operations, and machines through a unique architecture of performance and play.

Numerous different workshops and ateliers produced clothing, cookware, tools, and other types of hardware inside the Han's 210 small windowless rooms. Among these ateliers, textile and metal workers were in the majority, with a handful of them surviving to this day. These few still-functioning workshops are responsible for the occasional strange occurrence inside the Han–flames shooting up from metal furnaces and dramatically illuminating the dark corridors or mechanical sounds buzzing from looms and sewing machines, momentarily disturbing the otherwise silent corridors. These brief jolts of machinic, trade-related activities produce an unreal atmosphere within the calm, almost seclusive, hallways of the largely vacated Han. One gets the impression that the flashes of light, reflections of color, and piercing sounds from the machines are part of an artistic performance rather than the last remnants of bygone times. Inspired by this condition, the project proposes the reintroduction of textile and metal production to the Han, and, in doing so, transforms the building into a machinic performance space with the goal of attracting customers and spectators alike.

To serve this objective, parts of the building are upgraded, amended, and retrofitted with modern mills; looms; printers; spinning, combing, and dyeing machines; and new furnaces and metal presses. This equipment, the infrastructure necessary to operate it, and the products it produces are an integral part of the Performing Han's overall function and appearance. Alongside the everyday goods crafted, the Performing Han generates an excessive, or theatrical, overflow of materials

Fig. 2.53 Eric Jiancheng Gu & Xiaoqing Gua, Performing Han, rendering, Istanbul Studio, University of Pennsylvania Weitzman School of Design, 2019.

In this bird's-eye view of the Performing Han, the courtyard has been opened up and turned into a large gathering space where visitors can experience the luminous fabrics that decorate the space. The facades enclosing the courtyard have been decluttered and transformed into an animated theatrical setting by the movement of the colorful curtains.

that recasts the production of textile and metal goods as an educational and aesthetic event.

Encompassing and addressing various scales and senses, these performances are visible from the courtyard as well as on the inside. Large curtains woven from vivid, colorful fabrics billow within the gray arches of the Han. Spinning, spooling, and dyeing processes provide constant sound and motion. The building's aisles and large courtyard are transformed into a walkable stage where visitors can learn about the Han's different trades. On the inside, new flues and exhaust shafts are installed to accommodate the forges and furnaces, thickening and shaping the Han's existing walls, poches, and domes into sculpted artifacts that emanate a flickering reddish glow.

The Performing Han proposes an alternative reuse concept for preindustrial manufacturing spaces within historically significant buildings. In its prime, the Han provided a unique combination of manufacturing, commerce, and leisure space,

Figs. 2.54, 2.55 Above and opposite: Eric Jiancheng Gu & Xiaoqing Gua, Performing Han, renderings, Istanbul Studio, University of Pennsylvania Weitzman School of Design, 2019.

Customized looms are mounted below the arches, intertwining the Han's industrial history with its structure. The interlacing threads and the motion produced by the spooling transform the Han into a mechanical theater, in which a unique spatial and aesthetic performance plays out.

but industrialization has sorted these activities into separate spatial and programmatic realms, thus rendering the Han's typology obsolete. By (re)introducing the
performance aspect, the Büyük Valide Han regains a wider functionality and opens
up to other forms of entertainment without having to forfeit the qualities that have
characterized it since the days of the Silk Road. The orchestrated, performative
interplay between architecture, machine, craft, and merchandise illustrates how
new programmatic ecologies might emerge from outdated typologies and enrich the
postindustrial city.

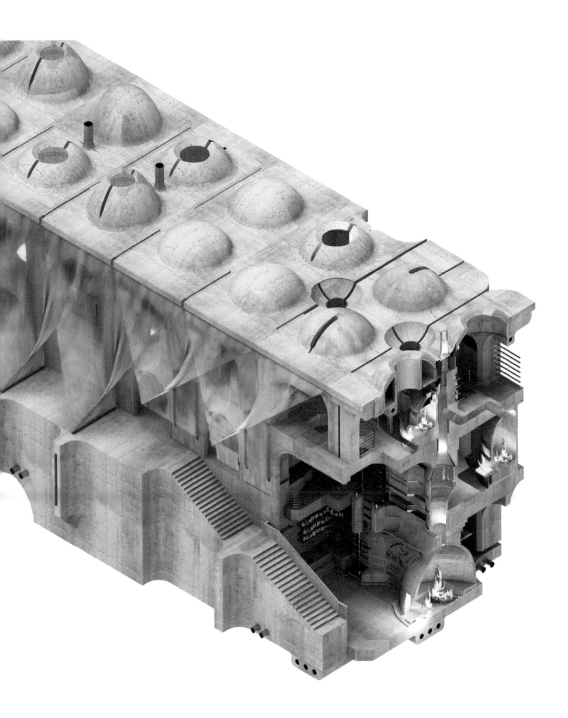

Figs. 2.56, 2.57 Above and opposite: Eric Jiancheng Gu & Xiaoqing Gua, Performing Han, renderings, Istanbul Studio, University of Pennsylvania Weitzman School of Design, 2019.

The Han becomes a large machine that integrates various looming, printing, and spinning devices. The cloth produced by the looms veils the courtyard facades in vibrant translucent hues. The character of the ancient structure is maintained and upgraded with prefabricated concrete components, furnaces, forging ovens, and other equipment needed for the traditional crafts practiced in the Han.

The Bird Sanctuary

In its current state, the courtyard of the Büyük Valide Han and its inner-facing facades are fragmented and cluttered by countless additions and the traces of repair work. These alterations have created myriad nooks and crannies that are used as rest stops and safe havens by native and migratory birds that pass through the city on their strenuous journey to the south. In the spring and fall, the courtyard comes alive with the hectic flutter and chirping of hundreds, if not thousands, of birds, highlighting yet another accidental quality of the Han: its function as a bird sanctuary. Seizing on this phenomenon, this project proposes a unique avian habitat by introducing new ornamental modifications to the facades that play on the historical and cultural motifs of the region and provide additional crevices for the birds to occupy.

The main courtyard of the Büyük Valide Han was originally the gravitational center of the bazaar. It served as both a religious gathering ground (to which the small Shia Mosque in the courtyard still attests) and as a space where merchants and traders could do business, rest, and engage in leisure activities. The programmatic and spatial mutuality between the Han's interior, where the shops and ateliers were located, and the public courtyard were indispensable to its overall functioning. The vanishing of the shops broke this mutual dependency and caused a partition between the building and courtyard, not only with respect to their spatial-programmatic continuity but also conceptually. As the vendors began to leave the building, the courtyard became isolated, filling up with parked cars, shack-like structures, overgrown dumpsters, and other residual objects. The demise of the courtyard and its separation from the Han building marks a curious shift from a dysfunctional human architecture toward that of a functional animal habitat.

The Bird Sanctuary builds on the chaotic layering of architectural enclosures that have been added to cover many of the open arches and maximize usable interior space. These ad hoc constructions are supplemented with new layers made from colorful and richly textured surfaces that attract birds and provide them with shelter. The vivid composite language and fragmented iconography of these layers derives from an intricate mix of Islamic tiling, traditional textile patterns, building leftovers, and organic matter, like moss and ivy, that has accumulated over time. The facades of the Han become once again legible and coherent, reestablishing a purposeful relationship between the facades and the courtyard. The courtyard is transformed into an urban garden where humans and animals share space and escape the hectic streets outside. From a distance, the refurbished exterior walls provide a colorful and intimate perimeter for the garden, up close, they reveal their cultural references and nonhuman inhabitants.

Animals of all kinds inhabit cities in large numbers and, unless they are domesticated and privately owned, they do so by appropriating urban architecture and

Fig. 2.58 Zoe Cennami & Margarida Mota, Bird Sanctuary, rendering,
Istanbul Studio, University of Pennsylvania Weitzman School of Design, 2019.

infrastructure. Cities are shaped by a symbiotic cohabitation of humans and animals, and yet, rarely does this important insight factor into the ways we think of or design cities. In fact, we strictly distinguish between buildings that serve humans and animals (zoos, animal shelters, aviaries, etc.). While this segregation is sensible regarding invasive or dangerous species, it makes little sense for animals that already mix and mingle with us on a daily basis, inhabiting the same structures we do, often without our knowledge. The Bird Sanctuary illustrates the potential benefits of overcoming such categorical distinctions with a hybrid architecture that highlights the cultural heritage of a place and benefits humans and nonhumans alike.

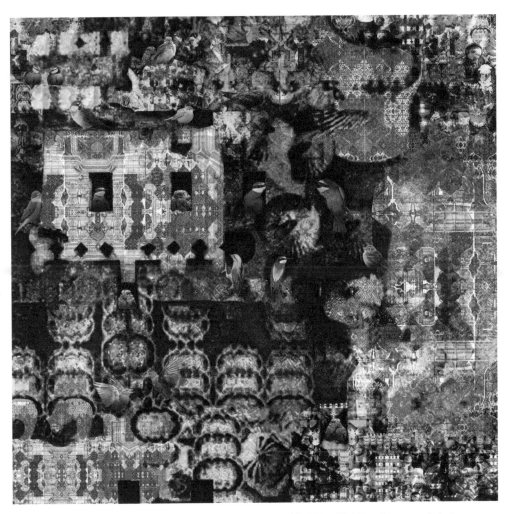

Figs. 2.59, 2.60 Above and opposite: Zoe Cennami & Margarida Mota, Bird Sanctuary, renderings, Istanbul Studio, University of Pennsylvania Weitzman School of Design, 2019.

Marked by nooks, cracks, patch-ups, and encrustations, the walls of the courtyard are used by native and migratory birds as an urban habitat. To support this phenomenon, new textural layers are added to the facade. Inspired by the rich colors and sumptuous fabrics that were once produced in the Han, the facade's mixture of cultural motifs and vibrant organic patterns is designed to attract birds.

Fig. 2.61 Bird Sanctuary, Zoe Cennami & Margarida Mota, rendering,
Istanbul Studio, University of Pennsylvania Weitzman School of Design, 2019.

The richly textured and colorful walls draw inspiration from local flora and fauna, as well as the traditional textile patterns and artisanal objects historically produced in the Han, creating a serene yet visceral atmosphere within the bird sanctuary.

Machinic Garden

Imperial Haliç Shipyard, Istanbul

The Imperial Haliç Shipyard is yet another example of a historically significant piece of urban architecture that has fallen from relevance and become a misfit in its current context. This landmark Ottoman facility has become incompatible with the demands and dynamics of the contemporary city. It faces a fate similar to many of the other inner-city industrial sites caught in the current of global postindustrial trends: namely, to be converted into predominantly commercial complexes and business parks with manufacturing operations relocated to the city's outskirts, where larger, more accessible sites can be found.

Unlike the Büyük Valide Han, this site is not nestled within a dense, labyrinthine shopping district, but instead occupies an open space at the entrance of the Golden Horn estuary, directly across from the historic peninsula and offering sweeping views of its many landmarks like the Hagia Sophia, Blue Mosque, and Süleymaniye Mosque. At its peak during the 16th and early 17th centuries, the Imperial Haliç Shipyard boasted more than 160 docks, along with numerous auxiliary buildings, schools, and military academies. However, as the Ottoman Empire's military dominance waned and the needs for civilian shipbuilding and maintenance services evolved, the old shipyard and its location were no longer sufficient. Today only three drydocks, a few cranes and other pieces of mechanical equipment, and a handful of distressed storage and repair buildings remain from what once was the embodiment of Ottoman naval pride.

The already vacated portions of the shipyard have become prime targets for the real estate industry based on their coveted waterfront locations and proximity to some of Istanbul's most popular neighborhoods. Following a rather generic formula, all too familiar to metropolitan areas worldwide, these sites have been restructured through a mixed-zone masterplan, calling for the typical array of office, retail, and leisure programs, designed to maximize profit margins and appeal to risk-averse business and franchise owners. In the process of this transformation, mechanical machinery and naval equipment deemed worthy of preservation are either given to museums or restored and kept on site as historical markers, alerting visitors to the industrial glory of bygone times within a safely curated park.[58]

This type of industrial site conversion has become the go-to approach in our postindustrial era, delivering at times compelling design solutions and successfully

Fig. 2.62 Imperial Haliç shipyard, Istanbul, 2019. (Photograph courtesy Ferda Kolatan.)
In this view of the shipyard's southernmost remaining drydock, the stepped walls of the repair basin blend seamlessly with the large retaining walls behind them to form a continuous urban "facade." An adorned wall niche, once used for ceremonial purposes, adds an intriguing contrast to the industrial language of the naval facility and the conventional office buildings above.

The **Imperial Haliç Shipyard** (Tersane-i Amire) was first established by Mehmed the Conqueror (Fatih Sultan Mehmet) in 1453, following the conquest of Constantinople by the Ottoman Turks. What began as a modest arsenal on the Galata bank of the Golden Horn (Haliç) had, by the early 16th century, grown into one of the largest naval bases in the Mediterranean. At the height of its expansion, the shipyard accommodated up to 160 individual docks, stretching over vast areas of the Golden Horn's northwestern edge. The facilities included numerous construction sites, warehouses, workshops, foundries, naval academies, schools, hospitals, and other resources for workers and their families. In the 18th century, the shipyard began its decline, mirroring the fate of the Ottoman fleet and, eventually, that of the Empire itself. Today only three repair basins and a few warehouses are left at the southernmost tip of the once sweeping navy yard. The three drydocks are still functional and are used primarily to service commercial vessels and the Istanbul ferries.

These remaining drydocks—built from 1796 to 1799, 1821 to 1825, and 1857 to 1870, respectively—are all near the original arsenal that Mehmed the Conqueror established across from the historic peninsula. The walls of the docks were constructed from limestone quarried in the Bosphorus region and mortar using volcanic ash from Mount Vesuvius. All drydocks feature an ornamented wall niche for ceremonial purposes, which adds a cultural component to the historical significance of the shipyard. Wedged in by the city's steady expansion toward the waterfront, the drydocks and the few auxiliary service buildings are the last reminders of a thriving shipbuilding industry that lasted centuries and was critical not only to the military and political power of the Ottomans but also the fate of Europe at large. Repair and maintenance operations are scheduled to cease as this last portion of the shipyard is to be relocated away from the inner city to free up the site for new development.

revitalizing moribund manufacturing sites with new programmatic features. However, rarely does this approach encompass scenarios in which the *machinic* elements are considered for types of productive architectural applications beyond their original purpose. The conversion of an industrial site should provide for a wider set of inquiries and speculations precisely because they pose such an intriguing problem to the city's transition from a place of material production to one of business, commerce, and leisure. If this transition can be understood as a hallmark of the 21st-century city, then the dysfunctional industrial site presents a pivotal locus to contemplate the nature of urban machines and explore how they could acquire new relevance instead of fading into the background of history.

The projects presented in this section take on these challenges in the context of the Imperial Haliç Shipyard. The removal of heavy manufacturing from inner cities is both necessary and sensible in the context of the broader picture, and these vacated sites offer an unrivaled opportunity to reflect on modernity's impact on the city. This is unlikely to happen by simply disposing of machines entirely or by relegating them to showcases or vaguely informative décor. The desire to reintegrate outdated technologies and their devices into the pulse of contemporary cities rests on the conviction that they possess a dormant capacity to originate new urban and architectural types even after their original intent or purpose has run its course.

The Machinic Garden is one such type. In the spirit of misfits and hybrids, the shipyard's distinct topographical location and history, its many fascinating mechanical tools and infrastructure, and the unique aesthetic features that have arisen from the layered accumulations of grease, algae, and rust are taken up as vital components for the design of the garden. In contrast to the neat and orderly approach of the developer projects and public parks that have taken over the freed-up banks of the Golden Horn, the Machinic Garden embraces and revels in the messy conditions of the shipyard and its surroundings. Rather than domesticating or idealizing industrial architecture, the garden explores the fourfold intersection between technological and historical components and synthetic and organic matter as a source for a new kind of active urban space.

Site: The Imperial Haliç Shipyard

From the busy waterways, aboard one of the smaller freight, fishing, or passenger boats that traverse the Golden Horn, the last surviving portion of the Imperial Shipyard comes into full view. Located inside a small bay next to the Atatürk bridge, the facility is wedged into a steep hillside on top of which rests the city, with the famous Galata Tower visible just behind it. A large, tiered, and slightly curved retaining wall pushes against the hill, creating the impression that one is facing an amphitheater couched strategically into a natural landscape or, perhaps, an ancient fortification wall guarding the city from unwanted intruders.

Fig. 2.63 Aerial View of the Imperial Haliç Shipyard, Istanbul, 2019. (Photograph courtesy Google Maps.)

The shipyard's three remaining drydocks cut deep into the coastline. Encircled by a multilane highway above, the shipyard is effectively isolated from the bustling nearby neighborhoods of Şişhane and Galata. This seclusion gives the site an enclosed, almost intimate quality, which the Machinic Garden capitalizes on.

The impression that one is facing a cultural edifice rather than an industrial shipyard is heightened by a unique feature common to all three drydocks but most pronounced in the one nearest to the bridge: a semicircular recess built into the back end of the basin walls. The portal-like shape of this niche and its classical detailing conjure visions of an ancient city gate or temple and create an intriguing contrast with the surrounding machinery. These niches were once used as a backdrop for ceremonial events, like the christening of new ships before launching them out to sea. Today, however, they appear curiously out of place and give the drydocks an ambiguous quality, particularly in contrast to the diametrically opposed caisson flood gates on the other end of the same basin.

Viewed from the water, the oval drydock walls merge seamlessly into the tiered retaining walls behind them, visually collapsing the space between, and forming what appears from afar as a continuous yet strangely misaligned facade with both structural and ornamental properties. An unexpected effect of this striking feature is a sense of urban interiority within the open shipyard, which is further accentuated by the abrupt transition from the facade-like retaining walls to the dispersion of buildings above and behind them. This horizontal sectioning of the site into two halves via the retaining walls reveals unexpected juxtapositions between the city's residential, commercial, and cultural buildings and the industrial machinery of the shipyard.

While the succession of steep walls dominates the view of the shipyard from the shores, from the street, the site has a different feel. From up here, one must first cross a multilane highway that encircles the facility, effectively cutting it off from the nearby pedestrian areas of Şişhane and Galata. After crossing the highway, one enters the upper section of the shipyard through a gate and follows a winding path down to the base where the drydocks and warehouses are located. This path provides a clear view of the three elongated basins, roughly arranged in a semicircle, their tips converging toward a distant point. In order to accommodate between one and two ships each, the repair basins cut deep into the hillside, blurring the boundaries between landscape and machinic architecture.

In and around the drydocks, the prevailing perception of the site changes once more. Numerous mechanical devices and infrastructural elements of different scales, functions, and eras occupy the shipyard grounds: flood gates, drainage pumps, water pipes, docking blocks and wedges, cranes, pressure washers, and

Fig. 2.64 Caisson gate, Imperial Haliç Shipyard, Istanbul, 2019.
(Photograph courtesy Ferda Kolatan.)

The shipyard is filled with curious machinic devices like the old caisson lock gate. Made from a large floating steel hull, the gate is controlled by the water level inside it. To lock it in place, the hull is filled to capacity; to open it up, the water is drained, making the gate float and allowing for ships to enter and exit the drydock. When viewed from inside the repair basin, which is usually accessible only to maintenance workers, the corroding gate appears rather alien and imposing. Water steadily escapes from various cracks, staining the stone of the drydock and covering it with bright green algae.

more. Some of this equipment is almost as old as the drydocks themselves and has deteriorated heavily, while some is newer and in better condition. The corroding metals have imparted a unique color palette upon the site, with hues of rusty browns, saturated oranges, and dark reds mixing with the vibrant greens of algae that has accumulated over the shipyard's watery surfaces.

Moreover, the drydocks themselves have a unique material history, built from blue Devonian limestone quarried in the Bosphorus region and Pozzolan mortar made from volcanic ash sourced from Mount Vesuvius.[59] In total, the shipyard is a manifestation of a wild array of different objects, colors, and textures, which are both organic and synthetic and bound together by mutual dependencies across scale, type, and function. The sensory effects of their multiple interactions–at times harmonious, at times discordant–combined with the backdrop of the urban facade sets the stage for the conceptual and material exploration of the Machinic Garden.

Figs. 2.65, 2.66 Mechanical equipment and drydock with wall niche, Imperial Haliç Shipyard, Istanbul, 2019. (Photograph courtesy Ferda Kolatan.)

Fig 2.65: Inside the workshops, various antiquated machines pay tribute to the industrial heritage of ship construction, repair, and maintenance. Surrounded by modern and fully functional machines, these artifacts do not appear out of place or obsolete but rather preserve the shipyard's history as palpable and immediate. Fig. 2.66: The ceremonial niches on the drydock walls create stark contrasts between their classical motifs, the functional language of the rounded dock, and the vivid colors of the corroding metals. The mixture of all these elements adds to the unique aesthetic of the shipyard.

Architecture of Flows and Accretions

Water, unsurprisingly, factors heavily in and around the shipyard and is a constant contributor to the material accretions that stain and shape the site. The Haliç estuary, from which the boats are pulled into the drydocks, is the most obvious example. Its salty water is filled with bacteria and pollutants and is the main cause of corroding metals and stained surfaces. In addition, the estuary is home to many aquatic organisms, like algae, that can visibly spread over the more porous materials in the shipyard. Water is also a tool in many of the daily operations of the facility, evidenced by the various pumps, tanks, shafts, channels, pipes, and other water-related infrastructure that covers the site. In fact, the majority of the shipyard's operations are contingent on controlling water one way or another–draining and filling the basins via overflow chambers, operating the drydock's hollow lock gates, running pressure pumps, cooling molten metals in the foundries, or sandblasting aging paint and marine residue off boat hulls.

Fig. 2.67 Andrew Matia, Machinic Garden, powder-print model, Istanbul Studio, University of Pennsylvania Weitzman School of Design, 2019.

In this project, the shipyard is transformed into a hydropower plant. The caisson lock gates function similarly to dams, controlling the waterflow into the repair basins, which now serve as penstocks. Two turbines with generators are installed in the basins, and the existing infrastructure surrounding the shipyard is repurposed to accommodate spillways, transformers, and powerhouses. The architecture of the drydock, with its distinctive stepped-basin shape and accompanying equipment, becomes an integral part of the new hydropower plant. The upper sections of the docks are redesigned to welcome visitors, incorporating bridges that span the docks to provide close-up views of the turbines. The garden embodies the dynamic interplay between nature and technology that propels the power-facility, resulting in a unique hybrid architecture. Carved into the existing drydocks and assembled from their residual parts, the Machinic Garden possesses a distinctly sculptural quality.

Fig. 2.68 Wenhao Xu, Machinic Garden, powder-print model,
Istanbul Studio, University of Pennsylvania Weitzman School of Design, 2019.

Here, an overflow basin is repurposed as an artificial cavern or grotto. Originally serving as a large
concrete tank between the drydocks, the basin was used to regulate and control water levels inside them.
Buried in the ground and hidden from view, the basin's interior walls have acquired a range of rusty and
mossy colors over the years. By selectively removing sections of the tank and adding new stairs, the
interior is made accessible to visitors. Additional water tanks containing dyed liquids, have been installed
to orchestrate the spillage, enriching the sensory experience with a symphony of sounds, hues, and
textures that define the shipyard. At the bottom, the liquids converge into a vibrant, cavernous pool—a
contemporary play on the picturesque garden grotto.

While these water-based processes are indispensable for the effective functioning of the shipyard, they also yield involuntary effects by incessantly eroding, displacing, moving, and depositing particles in and around the drydocks. Each of these processes utilizing water or other liquids triggers countless accidental events in the form of leakage, erosion, or sedimentation, all of which impact the soil and the material and structural properties of hard surfaces. The cumulative effects of these accidents may be considered as the regrettable yet inevitable byproducts of industrial production in need of cleaning up. This perception, however, overlooks a simple yet profound insight: namely, that in the aesthetic expressions of the residual, even toxic, depositions of matter come to light the complex material, technological, and environmental histories that ultimately comprise the shipyard.

In this sense, the mixed-up and textured accretions of algae, rust, grease, dirt, and wreckage can be considered as significant a historical record as the ornamented drydock niches or the antiquated naval equipment. In other words, the physical traces of overflows and spillages do not represent waste as much as the embodiment of centuries-old administrative and labor practices; material agencies; production

Fig. 2.69 Drydock Detail, Imperial Haliç shipyard, Istanbul, 2019. (Photograph courtesy Ferda Kolatan.)

The shipyard's ground is saturated with colors, patterns, and textures. These material conditions create a unique and visceral aesthetic that blends with and partially derives from the many objects and mechanical parts used in the facility. Hues of corroding metal stain the fissures in the concrete and rock, chipped paint particles deposit into the cracks of broken asphalt, erosion and weathering reveal strata mixing the organic with the synthetic. The Machinic Gardens incorporate these qualities into their design.

protocols; and the geological, vegetal, climatic, and hydrodynamic properties that forge the site. All these attributes and their myriad interactions combine into the entity we refer to as the Imperial Haliç Shipyard. The Machinic Garden cannot do justice to the complexity of the site, nor can it fix all the environmental hazards that have resulted from the heavy industrial use over long periods of time. What it can do is raise awareness of the fact that technology, architecture, and nature are forever entwined, and that this entwinement expresses itself in hybrid forms, textures, and colors. The aesthetic of the Machinic Garden is inseparable from its material histories.

Fig. 2.70 Emily Sun, Machinic Garden, rendered photomontage, Istanbul Studio, University of Pennsylvania Weitzman School of Design, 2019.

The drydock's ceremonial niche and the retaining wall behind it become the backdrop for a new performative architecture. The painterly effects produced by existing flow patterns and residual matter around the drydock are enhanced. Distorted symmetries, vaguely referencing the classicist niche, carve a highly ornamented, cavernous space into one side of the stepped repair basin. Existing water infrastructure is repurposed to stain the walls of the shipyard and irrigate plants that grow over the structure. The drydock takes on a new role as a contemporary folly, an urban ruin hiding below the datum line of the city.

Performing Machines and Painterly Gardens

A constant flowing, spouting, and dripping of water, both from the sea and from within the shipyard, echoes throughout the site, perpetually eroding matter and depositing myriads of particles into the soil, metal, concrete, and rock elements of the facility. Vivid pigmentations accumulate in a striking alchemical patina, displaying strange painterly effects, textured figurations, and radiant patterns of color. Deeply saturated greens from algae and moss cover the stone walls of the old drydocks with a soft, tissue-like layer; rich hues of red and orange invoke the corroding metals and rusty tools scattered around the navy yard; saline sedimentation marks the ground with bright patches; puddles of water, slick with oil and grease, catch the sky's colors and mirror the mechanical limbs of machines nearby.

Fig. 2.71 Emily Sun, Machinic Garden, powder-print model, Istanbul Studio, University of Pennsylvania Weitzman School of Design, 2019.

The sidewalls of the drydock are thickened to accommodate cavernous new interiors. The topographical features of the stepped walls are projected into the basin interior to create a folly in which tectonic, sculptural, and painterly elements hybridize into an architectural fantasy. Dyed water stains the dock, blurring boundaries between the effects of deliberate artistic acts and those of natural processes.

The excesses of industrialization and their cumulative effects have transformed the Imperial Haliç Shipyard into a vast canvas.

Through deliberate manipulations of its existing water ecologies, the shipyard becomes a stage for organic, mechanical, and synthetic interactions. Water from the estuary is pumped into remote areas of the site, turning pressure chambers into moody grottoes, irrigating the shipyard floors to grow plants in unexpected places, and carving new patterns into the earth like prehistoric ornaments. Converted plumbing pipes and water channels gush out liquids infused with organic pigmentation, cascading down the steep terrain and washing over the stepped drydock walls like exotic waterfalls. The liquid colors blend with mossy textures and viscous vegetation, staining the shipyard's architecture with intricate and wavy shapes.

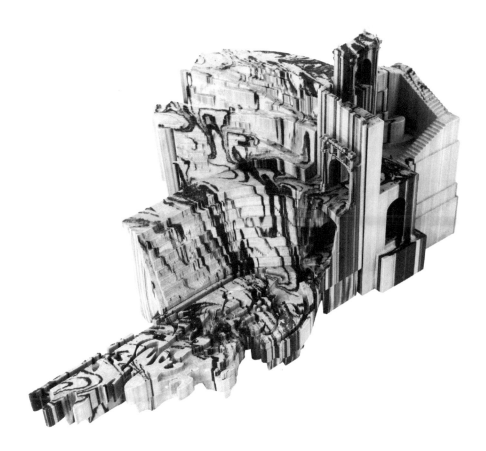

Fig. 2.72 Christian Cueva, Machinic Garden, powder-print model, Istanbul Studio, University of Pennsylvania Weitzman School of Design, 2019.

The upward motion from the repair basin to the retaining wall creates a continuous promenade that connects the city with the bottom of the drydock. The ceremonial niche is transformed into a gate, from which a staircase leads to the sidewalk outside the shipyard. Flowing colors, common to the shipyard, cover the site and create intricate patterns reminiscent of ebru painting.

The dock gates are manipulated to leak water into artificial reservoirs, resembling strangely picturesque ponds amidst the decaying industrial site.

To simulate these liquid effects, the projects borrow analog techniques from the traditional Turkish art form of ebru and integrate them with digital modeling. In ebru, dye is pulled over the surface of water with a brush or stick to create images with symmetrical patterns, delicate figurations, and abstract flows. The affinity between ebru painting and the water-based material formations and colorations in the shipyard plays on one of the core ideas of hybrid architecture: to combine cross-categorical and cross-scalar associations into a diverse yet coherent design expression. Viewed from above, the gardens resemble large, distorted ebru paintings that merge with the site's topographical features, flowing over existing building parts and objects, and fusing cultural, machinic, and natural features. Up close, they reveal new aesthetic experiences afforded by the dynamic techniques of water painting and encourage spontaneous participation in the varied performances of the garden.

Fig. 2.73 Agata Jakubowska, Machinic Garden, rendering, Istanbul Studio, University of Pennsylvania Weitzman School of Design, 2019.

The shipyard's surfaces exude a mesmerizing viscosity, a remarkable blend of organic and machine-infused elements that together create a "synthetic nature." In an enigmatic fusion, terrestrial and aquatic flora intertwine with the decaying structures of the shipyard. To explore these conditions up-close, strategic cuts are made into the basins, and existing waterlines are redirected to nourish the plants and mosses growing over their weathered limestone surfaces. These incisions yield a collection of chunky artifacts, transforming the drydock into a hybrid object-landscape with both botanical and mechanical features.

The Garden

In many ways, gardens are already hybrid entities in which the forces of nature fuse with the agencies of the gardener to produce altered, refined, or entirely new organic artifacts. As such, the laying out and cultivation of a garden is a deeply collaborative act where humans, soil, plants, and other environmental factors operate within a tight reciprocal ecology. These manifold associations and entanglements with nature, culture, and fiction distinguish the garden from the urban park, which has become the preferred nomenclature for modern recreational space. Unlike the garden, the park's relationship to questions regarding nature and culture is more straightforward, driven largely by statistical calculations, property speculation, and other pragmatic and administrative considerations. As a result, parks often follow formulaic rules, emphasizing outdoor activities on lawns and fields, and rarely invest in a deeper exploration of the concept of nature in the context of postindustrial cities.

Fig. 2.74 Sihan Zhu, Machinic Garden, rendered photomontage,
Istanbul Studio, University of Pennsylvania Weitzman School of Design, 2019.

An array of painted concrete components is integrated into the hill and functions as a walkable sculpture. Some of the components serve as retention pools and are connected to the water systems of the shipyard. Others have built-in cavities that can be explored by visitors. The strict boundaries between the concrete, soil, and plants are renegotiated by the continuity of color and the ebru patterning.

The garden evokes a very different set of associations and conjures up images from a much wider thematic and temporal range. Since the beginning of human story-telling, the garden has been imbued with magical powers and functioned much like a projective canvas for human fears and desires.[60] The need to carve out and maintain a liminal space between the city and the "wild" is deeply engrained in the human psyche and has influenced artistic imagination since antiquity, while taking a distinctly modern twist in the 19th century.[61] During the baroque and rococo periods, pleasure-gardens became a popular destination, luring visitors into fabulous fictitious constructions, intricately mixing elements from nature, history, and fantasy into novel forms of entertainment.[62] Gardens also have a long tradition as spaces of learning and experimentation, as is evidenced by the monastic and medicinal gardens that served as research laboratories during medieval times.

For all the above reasons, the term *garden* captures the finer points and ambitions of the projects on these pages, namely, to evoke a public arena that seeks to explore the cultural theme of nature in its latest iteration as a technological hybrid. In

Fig. 2.75 Drydock Detail, Imperial Haliç Shipyard, Istanbul, 2019.
(Photograph courtesy Ferda Kolatan.)

Close up, the effects of weathering and industrial processes on the stone surfaces of the basin are revealed. Algae, moss, corrosion, and spills have accumulated into a thickly textured patina saturated with colors ranging from lively greens to moody reds. In these hybrid accretions of synthetic and natural matter, the age-old processes and practices of the naval industry and their environmental impact become aesthetically manifest.

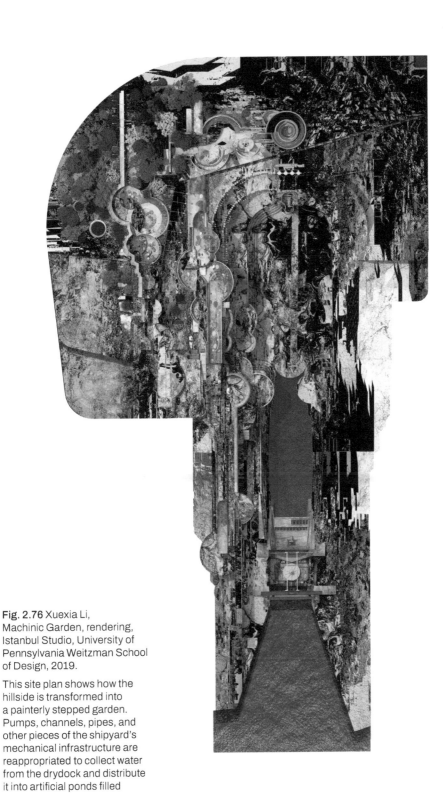

Fig. 2.76 Xuexia Li,
Machinic Garden, rendering,
Istanbul Studio, University of
Pennsylvania Weitzman School
of Design, 2019.

This site plan shows how the
hillside is transformed into
a painterly stepped garden.
Pumps, channels, pipes, and
other pieces of the shipyard's
mechanical infrastructure are
reappropriated to collect water
from the drydock and distribute
it into artificial ponds filled
with pigments.

the age of the Anthropocene, distinctions between nature and technology are no longer meaningful, as those categories have been forged into an altogether different amalgamation, one marked by ambiguities and contradictions.[63] In its current condition, the shipyard exemplifies anthropogenic diffusions between nature, culture, and technology, rendering them visually and viscerally accessible to the visitor. In its decaying machinery and polluted environment, the excesses of industrial technology–their uncontrollable and accidental discharges, and their effects on all matter, organic or manufactured–become manifest.

The Machinic Garden deals with these manifestations directly but explicitly refrains from common practices of sanitizing former industrial sites into benign pedestrian recreation zones. Instead, what is proposed here, is to consider these types of sites and their conditions of decay and pollution as the pre-requisite condition for the possibility of a synthetically re-enchanted nature. Since modernity, technology's relationship to nature has often been posited as one of dominance and subjugation for material and/or scientific gains. The

Figs. 2.77, 2.78 Above and opposite: Xuexia Li, Machinic Garden, renderings, Istanbul Studio, University of Pennsylvania Weitzman School of Design, 2019.

The painterly effects produced by analog water-marbling techniques are here digitally simulated and enhanced (Fig. 2.78). Collection pools are integrated into the drydock basins, where water mixes with organic pigments to create new patterns. The drydocks become artificial ponds and the landscape around the shipyard takes on the qualities of a synthetically "enchanted" garden.

Enlightenment's establishment of *reason* and scientific inquiry as the only valid forms of engaging the world has radically altered nature's cultural meaning, and turned it into a largely passive object to be studied, harnessed, and exploited. This impoverishment of nature into a mere resource via technological means gave rise to the notion of the "disenchantment of the world" in the early 20th century.[64]

Perhaps then, in an unexpected twist, the means of disenchantment have come full circle and the eerie specter of a nature-machine, rather than revealing a truth about the world, has drawn a veil over it, making it ever more mysterious. This realization leads us into uncharted territories and demands paradigmatic changes in our outlook toward the world. The belief in the possibility that this perilous condition can be overcome by technological fixes or halting and reversing these hazardous effects via environmental protection, regulation, and safeguarding is

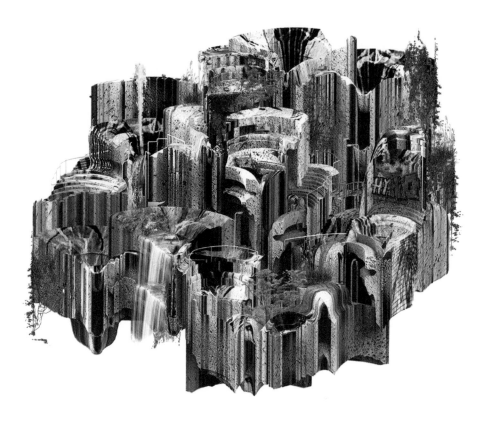

Figs. 2.79, 2.80 Above and opposite: Sihan Zhu, Machinic Garden, renderings, Istanbul Studio, University of Pennsylvania Weitzman School of Design, 2019.

The semicircular shapes of the drydocks are an additional motif in this digital ebru painting and rendered to suggest three-dimensional landscaping. The new garden architecture derives from the formal qualities of ebru and is implemented as a terracing landscape comprising a series of painted concrete components.

ultimately rooted in the same hegemonic stance that has propped up our asymmetrical attitude toward the material world since the early days of Modernity.

The Machinic Garden might not offer concrete solutions for the environmental problems that face the postindustrial city and the planet at large, far from it, but it does attempt to recover a bit of the magic nature once held before being demystified, classified, and resourced in the age-long processes of scientific inquiry. Magic, that is, not as a belief in the supernatural or as the heralding call to turn back the clocks to premodern times but as a means of repositioning vis-a-vis nature, of breaking with the anthropocentric hubris that has dominated Western thought, and encouraging a sense of nervous wonder and even empathy with the nonhuman world. There hardly seems a more appropriate time and place to explore these questions than in the countless industrial facilities that have entered their final phase of serviceability like the Imperial Haliç Shipyard. Once the noise of the daily operations ceases and the facilities become useless, the arcane and trivial entwinements between machines and nature come into focus.

Fig. 2.81 Xuexia Li, Machinic Garden, rendering,
Istanbul Studio, University of Pennsylvania Weitzman School of Design, 2019.

This view of the transformed drydock shows how the stepped sidewalls of the basin have been altered and reorganized into smaller retention ponds. The spillage, grease, and residue from the shipyard's repair and maintenance processes are incorporated into the garden's aesthetic.

Fig. 2.82 Wenhao Xu, Machinic Garden, rendering,
Istanbul Studio, University of Pennsylvania Weitzman School of Design, 2019.

The garden unfolds as an enchanting industrial grotto, where buried tanks, overflow basins, spillways, and other mechanical water retainers create an array of cavernous spaces. The interiors of these devices create an unfamiliar architectural experience for visitors, while the spill-water takes on a performative role as a kind of waterfall, adding a touch of whimsy to the scene.

NOTES

58 Examples of old industrial equipment being turned into exhibits are plenty. The Zeche Zollverein in Essen, Germany, is one such example. The former coal mining complex was declared a heritage site in 2001 and subsequently transformed under a masterplan by OMA into a mix of business, education, and art-related programs. Notable industrial machines like the Doppelbock winding tower over Shaft 12 were restored and presented as open-air sculptures. A more recent example is the Domino Park in Brooklyn, designed by James Corner Field Operations, which showcases industrial equipment as artifacts: "The 5-acre riverfront park showcases the history of an iconic industrial waterfront site by integrating over 30 large-scale salvaged relics, including 21 original columns from the Raw Sugar Warehouse, gantry cranes, screw conveyors, bucket conveyors, and syrup tanks into an interpretive and educational 'Artifact Walk,' https://www.fieldoperations.net.

59 To read more about the history and details of the drydocks see the official site of the public sea transportation services in Istanbul (Şehir Hatları), https://www.sehirhatlari.istanbul/en/sirketi-hayriye/tersanei-amire-396.

60 The association of gardens with magical or divine powers goes back to the earliest myths. From the "garden of the gods" with trees bearing jewels as fruits in *The Epic of Gilgamesh* (~2000 BCE) and the "Garden of Eden" in the Book of Genesis to modern folk and fairy tales by the Brothers Grimm, Hans Christian Andersen, or Lewis Carroll, the garden is a space in which the *real* (expressed as nature) mixes with the imaginary.

61 Leo Marx has written beautifully about the pastoral as a medium for the aestheticization of industrialized landscapes in his seminal book *The Machine in the Garden*. The projects in "Machinic Garden" represent a play on Marx and the estranging effects of technology on concepts of nature and vice versa. Leo Marx, *The Machine in the Garden* (New York: Oxford University Press, 1964).

62 An embodiment of this can be found in the architectural folly, which took on different guises in the palace gardens of the 17th to 19th centuries. Resembling classical ruins, chinoiseries, Ottoman pavilions, grottoes, and other similar structures, the folly was more than just a backdrop for picnics. As interactive spaces, they transformed into literal stages, where plays were performed, immersing the participants in distant lands and cultures, and fostering a sense of wonder and imagination.

63 The perplexing hybridizations between nature and technology have sparked bewilderment, alarm, and intellectual speculation long before the term *Anthropocene* entered our vocabulary. From Martin Heidegger's notion of nature as a "standing reserve" to Bruno Latour's "quasi-objects" and Timothy Morton's more recent "hyperobjects," many thinkers of the 20th and early 21st have attempted to come to terms with the profoundly destabilizing impact of modern technology on both "real" nature and our ideas of what constitutes it.

64 The sociologist Max Weber popularized the notion of the "disenchantment of the world" in a lecture delivered in 1918 at the conclusion of the First World War. According to Weber, secular modern society, with its emphasis on scientific reason and rationalization, had entered an era of disenchantment, devaluing the more traditional and religious belief systems that governed premodern societies.

Figs. 2.83, 2.84 Above and next spread: Andrew Homick, *Machinic Garden*, rendered photomontage and renderings, Istanbul Studio, University of Pennsylvania Weitzman School of Design, 2019.

The drydock merges with the retaining walls to create a rounded facade-like element (Fig. 2.83). Behind the drydock walls are cavernous chambers that function as concealed follies. Blending the real with the imaginary, these follies are represented as freestanding pavilions with fictional exteriors (Fig. 2.84). Their irregular shapes are produced by projecting the outlines of adjacent buildings and machines onto the drydock walls, and by sectioning the pavilions at oblique angles. The follies' interiors are adorned with colorful tiles that combine traditional Turkish motifs with abstract patterns derived from the distortions of the projected outlines.

CAIRO

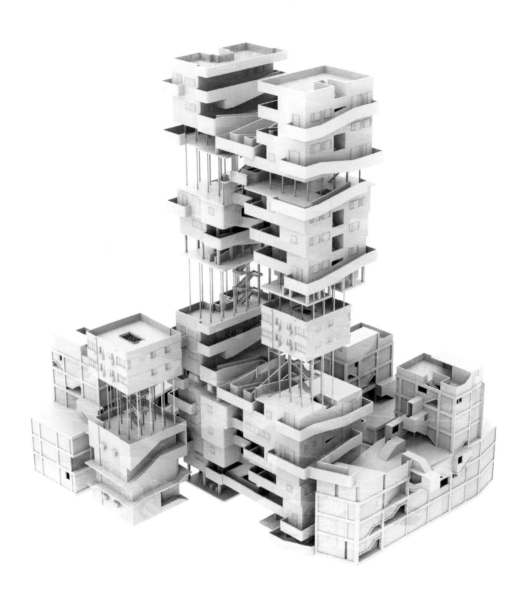

Fig. 3.1 Informal Assets Cairo, rendering,
Cairo Studio, University of Pennsylvania Weitzman School of Design, 2016.

Misfit typologies frequently observed in Cairo's informal settlements are stacked into a fictitious vertical assembly. Upon closer examination, the incomplete and residual aspects of these buildings have unexpected resemblances to modern architectural marvels. "Real Fictions" explores how value is assigned to formal characteristics, and how these values can be potentially reversed.

138

Cairo

Real Fictions

The legendary city on the banks of the Nile is the second site for our exploration of the untapped potential for hybrid architecture inherent in misfit urban constellations. In many respects, Cairo and Istanbul are remarkably similar–vibrant megacities with ancient and fabled pasts, rich in splendor and cultural diversity, and brimming with the tensions and contradictions deeply ingrained in their buildings and streetscapes. Both cities also struggle with the adverse effects of the profound socioeconomic and cultural transformations experienced by metropolitan areas globally in the 21st century, such as unmitigated growth, overpopulation, poverty and inequality, traffic congestion, and environmental degradation.

In the cases of Istanbul and Cairo, these issues are further compounded by the concurrent and often turbulent intersections of preindustrial, modern, and postindustrial influences and practices. Without falling into tired stereotypes of "East" and "West," the diverse histories expressed by these intersections are more apparent in these cities than in most of their Western counterparts. Here, the architectural remnants of bygone epochs seem less confined to specific areas and more ingrained into the general fabric of the cities. Notably, the progressive forces of modernity have never exerted full command over places like Cairo and Istanbul; instead, they engage in a continual negotiation with the cities' histories. Misfit accretions comprising architectural and urban components are often the tangible result of these negotiations.

While the Istanbul section, "Unscripted Immediacies of Past, Present, and Future," primarily addresses the contradictory architectural conditions that emerge from the unlikely adjacencies spawned by historical overlaps, this section examines contradictions of a different megalopolitan kind. Here, the focus is not on specific buildings or sites that have accumulated mixed characteristics over long periods, which are then explored for their potential to generate unique and historically inflected architectural hybrids. Instead, projects in the Cairo section aim to identify misfits produced by rapid urban expansion and the forces and tensions that accompany it. Similar to the projects developed for Istanbul, which aimed to establish a productive territory for design innovation based on historical overlaps and unlikely adjacencies, the Cairo projects perceive ever-accelerating urban growth as a catalyst for misfits and, consequently, untapped opportunities for hybrid design.

The design approach employed in "Real Fictions" addresses two phenomena produced by uncontrolled urban growth, particularly prevalent in Cairo. The first phenomenon, detailed in the "Informal Assets" chapter, pertains to the informal settlements that occupy significant portions of the city; while the second, detailed in the "Over/Under" chapter, concerns the disruptive effects caused by the landing zones of large vehicular bridges on the inner city. Both phenomena pose severe practical, economic, and health-related hazards for residents, impede the proper functioning of the city, and are generally considered detrimental to Cairo's aesthetic appearance and appeal. In the absence of comprehensive and actionable plans to address these issues, more incremental and ad hoc approaches–without reliance on governmental resources, political goodwill, or commercial interests and lobbying– are being deployed by local populations.

"Real Fictions," positing the inherent value in these interventions, presents tactical designs that reframe informal architecture as a productive and even desirable scenario. Real fictions are thus spin-offs of these interventions, employing and emphasizing the existing vernacular modes of design and construction. Existing structures are altered just enough to conjure new programmatic and functional scenarios, and prompt us to reconsider our deep-seated perceptions, convictions, and prejudices with respect to what constitutes a building's architectural and cultural value.

The following chapter, "Informal Assets," contains three subchapters, each set within one of metropolitan Cairo's vast informal settlements. The first subchapter comprises the Informal Assets Catalogue and focuses on Manshiyat Naser, which, along with all of Cairo's informal settlements, is replete with ingenious interventions that have transformed disadvantageous conditions into assets. These assets are presented as such in a fictitious real estate catalogue, in which unlikely parallels are drawn to acclaimed architectural precedents, and qualities typically viewed as emblems of poverty, dysfunction, and decay are reconceived as hot commodities in the real estate market.

The tone of the Informal Assets Catalogue may come across as somewhat light-hearted in relation to the severe challenges facing these communities. However, the projects in the catalogue are far from indifferent to the serious health and safety concerns that plague informal settlements, or the severe socioeconomic disadvantages caused by the social stigma and marginalization of places like Manshiyat Naser as irredeemable "slums." On the contrary, the objective of the "Informal Assets" chapter as a whole is to demonstrate that the large-scale demolition and gentrification of these neighborhoods is not the only solution to their municipal neglect. Rather, a low-key approach aimed at utilizing and retrofitting dilapidated structures provides a practical and actionable recourse for improving buildings and living conditions in informal settlements.

Ezbet Khairallah, another large informal district in Cairo, has provided an intriguing example for the second subchapter. The neighborhood is intersected by a massive highway known as the Ring Road, further exacerbating the hardships faced by this already marginalized local community. However, even under these circumstances, surprising and innovative episodes of architectural intervention have taken place. These clever acts of defiance are driven entirely by the initiative of local residents. The project in the third subchapter takes up the Gabkhana, a historic yet largely forgotten ammunitions depot in Istabl Antar.

The second chapter of Cairo projects, "Over/Under," deals with the detrimental effects of large vehicular infrastructure. Situated along the Nile River, Cairo relies on its many bridges to connect different parts of the sprawling metropolis and facilitate travel in a city severely lacking sufficient options for public transportation. The suffocating traffic conditions in Cairo, however, are not the focus of this study. Instead, "Over/Under" focuses on the components of these bridges that present obstacles and unexpected encounters for pedestrians as they are forced to navigate around them, often under hazardous circumstances.

From a distance, structural trusses, piers, cables, foundation walls, roadways, on- and off-ramps, overhangs, and abutments are essential to the bridge as a legible and coherent structure. However, up close, these same components often appear decontextualized and out of place. They emerge in unexpected moments, introducing scales, forms, and geometries that can have an estranging effect on the familiar pedestrian experience of the inner city. "Over/Under" captures these moments of urban estrangement, presenting a series of eclectic autonomous artifacts with additional programmatic functions and the ability to precipitate spontaneous cultural activities.

Three vehicular bridges spanning the Nile River and Zamalek Island provide the material for this exploration. These bridges cut through densely populated areas and offer numerous opportunities for hybrid design above, below, and adjacent to their landings. Alongside the renderings of free-floating objects, a collection of realistic interior and detail renderings demonstrates how the dark, inhospitable, and often perilous spaces around bridge foundations can be converted into valuable urban architecture. These spaces, squeezed into hidden and inaccessible pockets, tunnels, and recesses, are frequently overlooked, or go completely unnoticed, by the city's inhabitants. In the spirit of misfit conversions, "Over/Under" understands these spaces as belonging to a de facto public realm, underutilized and ready for its potential to be unlocked through hybrid design interventions.

Above all else, "Real Fictions," targets the largely arbitrary nature of how architecture is classified as good or bad. These classifications have profound implications not only for buildings themselves but also for the communities that live in and organize their lives around them. These categories can determine the survival or decline of a specific building, structure, or entire neighborhood. A building's appearance and its aesthetic features play a crucial role in these assessments, regardless of who is making them–planners, architects, politicians, or ordinary pedestrians. To be considered an asset or desirable, a building must meet certain standards that we, the inhabitants of global postindustrial cities, seem to reflexively agree upon. At the most basic level, a building should, for instance, appear finished; this is not the case for most in informal settlements. It must also be coherent as a whole, much like a bridge that rises majestically from a distance, even though, up close, that same bridge may be experienced in awkward fragments, out of context and out of scale.

While the broader circumstances that contribute to bad or undesirable architecture being classified as such are rarely architectural in nature, these circumstances are nevertheless physically manifest in buildings. Conversely, the appearance and aesthetics of buildings influence our perception of what defines good or bad architecture in the first place. The Cairo projects are situated at the intersection of these two concepts. The projects devised for Manshiyat Naser, Ezbet Khairallah, and Istabl Antar, along with those deriving from the bridges along the Nile, unpack some of Cairo's most egregious urban problems and examine them from a different angle. Viewed from this alternative perspective, bad architecture, whether associated with disadvantaged communities or inadequately planned infrastructural projects, can be redeemed. It can be valued not only for its functional aspects as a structural or programmatic unit but also for its ability to embody, in unique and innovative ways, the often overlooked yet authentic cultural aspects of a specific site and place.

Fig. 3.2 Yi Yan & Siqi Wang, Over/Under, repurposed bridge segment, rendering.
Cairo Studio, University of Pennsylvania Weitzman School of Design, 2017.

"Over/Under" explores the dormant potential of bridges to generate new urban architecture. Here, a bridge segment in a populous area is repurposed into a public forum for pedestrians.

Informal Assets

Cairo's Informal Settlements

An asset can be many different things in different circumstances. From tangible assets like land, property, precious metals, stocks, bonds, and cash to intangible ones like trademarks, copyrights, and intellectual property, the term *asset* is used rather broadly to refer to both material and immaterial entities with some quantifiable value. People can also be considered as assets.

Given these definitions, informal housing is unlikely to ever be considered an asset unless, of course, it sits on valuable land, in which case it will be slated for demolition to pave the way for new development. In such cases, the value of the asset is determined by the land value after the removal of any existing built structures. Since the mid-20th century, complete demolition and redevelopment has become the preferred municipal approach for dealing with informal settlements, but the negative effects of gentrification on poor and lower-income residents, who comprise the majority of these settlements' inhabitants, are severe and well documented. Considering the widespread presence of these settlements in and around Cairo, and the significant population whose livelihoods revolve around them, it would be negligent not to explore how architectural interventions can address and change the stigmatization associated with the informal. These interventions involve devising design tactics and representational techniques that can present the informal in a new light, as compelling, useful, and full of potential. Under these circumstances, the informal can indeed become an asset.

To locate the value of an asset not in terms of competition and profit margins but rather mutuality, exchange, and collaborative action, all of which are key factors for the impromptu and improvisational economic and ecological functions that drive informal settlements, is one of the central tenets of the projects that follow.

The projects in this section propose various architectural interventions by targeting the unfinished, residual, and ad hoc features often associated with informal or extralegal housing. Instead of being dismissed for their unorthodox construction and lack of safety and aesthetic appeal, these buildings and components are regarded here as dormant assets. Although many of these structures do pose genuine risks to their inhabitants, which should neither be minimized nor ignored, they also showcase rather ingenious design solutions that have emerged in direct response to the numerous challenges facing informal communities. Largely abandoned by federal and local governing bodies, and with no sufficient logistical, financial, or infrastructural support, the architecture of informal settlements relies heavily on communal efforts, peer networks, and the clever and opportunistic utilization of available building methods and materials.

Fig. 3.3 Informal Assets, rendering,
Cairo Studio, University of Pennsylvania Weitzman School of Design, 2016.

Informal Assets Catalogue

The projects presented in "Informal Assets" visualize and celebrate the bottom-up practices that underlie informal construction as bona fide design expressions. The odd structures, compositions, and details that arise from limited means, resources, and the absence of top-down planning and oversight are recognized as valuable architectural contributions in themselves. These contributions not only benefit their own communities but also showcase how the intelligence, robustness, and versatility of improvisational design tactics can foster new types of architecture as well as a distinct formal language. The programmatic, practical, and functional peculiarities that characterize informal buildings are embraced for their innovative approach to problem-solving and their unique aesthetic appeal.

To advertise this architecture of informal assets, a fictitious real estate catalogue has been created. The catalogue features a curated selection of buildings, infra-structural components, and larger urban conglomerations derived from the combination of individual structures. All examples are based on existing conditions and have been directly modeled after the diverse building stock found in Cairo's informal settlements. Specific design features have been chosen and customized to develop new types by leveraging the limited resources available to the residents and addressing their needs for more adaptable, multifunctional, and unconventional urban setups. What are typically considered as deficiencies and imperfections are interpreted here as distinctive characteristics that are advertised as sought-after and desirable attributes for a dynamic mix of live-, work-, and leisure-related programs. Consisting exclusively of black-and-white renderings, the catalogue emphasizes the often-overlooked formal idiosyncrasies of these structures and promotes them as authentic expressions of an "informal style." In an ironic twist, this style reveals a surprising resemblance to an altogether different, and much more revered, architectural style, that of classical modernism.

Ultimately, all commercial real estate catalogues are geared to sell a fantasy. Carefully crafted to cater to the customer's preconceived or conditioned notions of real estate value, the images found in these catalogues are less about accurately portraying a property's physical attributes and more about constructing a credible fiction that entices buyers. This fiction needs to be tangible enough to capture attention and create a desire to own the property, but it must also conform to the familiar standards of the market and not come across as too different or unique. The Informal Assets Catalogue serves as a playful commentary on branding and advertising practices commonly employed to attract potential buyers to real estate investments. Traditionally, these practices follow an unimaginative formula: glossy renderings of upscale apartment buildings, residential towers, and gated communities with extravagant names designed to evoke a sense of luxury, safety, and sophistication. These portrayals often consist of predictably pristine exterior views, stylish yet sterile interiors, and lavish amenities such as rooftop terraces, green spaces, gyms, and impeccably empty swimming pools. After all, while uniqueness and individuality may be appealing to some, from an asset perspective, these qualities pose a risk to resale values. The monotonous sameness of these images is reflected in banal property renderings, generic site photographs, and clichéd catchphrases, all of which align with the prevailing global trend in real estate advertising.[65]

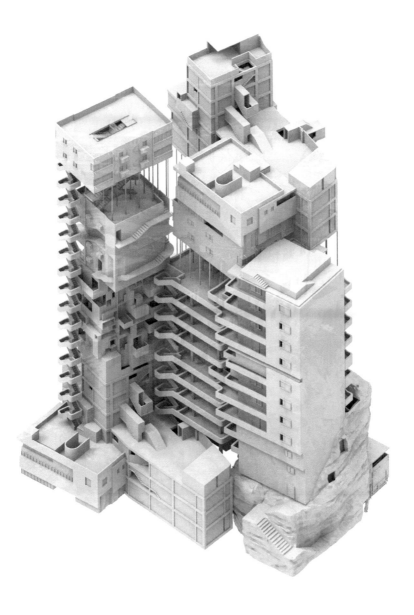

Fig. 3.4 Informal Assets, rendering,
Cairo Studio, University of Pennsylvania Weitzman School of Design, 2016.

In response to this prevailing trend, and with a keen awareness of the distinct nature of its featured properties, the projects featured in the Informal Assets Catalogue present a counternarrative. Instead of showcasing idyllic residential complexes, complete with golf courses, luxury franchises, and gated security, this collection presents a rather bewildering assortment of faux modernist villas, conjoined mansions, urban barns, conveyor houses, rock dwellings, and other hybrids assembled from the vast repertoire of strange combinatorial modes operating in informal settlements. While in Cairo, images of lofty new developments attempt to entice the more affluent population to leave congested urban neighborhoods and settle in the rapidly growing satellite communities sprawling across the desert, "Informal Assets" promotes an incremental revitalization of the inner city.[66]

To clarify, the argument here does not call for a simplistic or naïve dissolution of deeply ingrained social and structural boundaries through a set of architectural hybrids. Such a monumental task would certainly require extensive collaborative efforts, financial means, and political will, reaching far beyond the realm of design alone. However, what design can accomplish, is to identify legitimate opportunities in impoverished buildings and transform them into architectural assets. This process leads us inevitably into the realm of speculation, conjecture, and representation. However, as real estate advertisements demonstrate, architecture as a commodity is inherently contingent on narratives, and narratives are inherently malleable. The construct of the asset is but an expression of this manipulation, designed to favor certain metrics of success and prosperity while rejecting others. Repeated consistently enough, these narratives tend to be accepted as reality, eventually materializing as self-fulfilling prophecies.

The Informal Assets Catalogue is not intended to replace existing narratives but rather to serve as a somewhat unruly companion to the dominant fictions that shape cities with significant informal settlements such as Cairo. The images presented

Fig. 3.5 Aerial view of the informal settlements at the foot of Mokattam Mountain in Manshiyat Naser, Cairo, 2022. (Photograph courtesy Google Maps.)

in the catalogue may not necessarily encourage the wholesale transformation of informal neighborhoods into thriving and prosperous communities, at least not according to the standards set by the prevailing narratives. However, they do bring attention to the productive potential of the diverse tensions generated by municipal neglect. This is the narrative that the "Informal Assets" chapter aims to convey.

The catalogue showcases a collection of semi-fictitious properties and urban artifacts conceived as assets and derived from the odd conglomerations and convergences mentioned above. These assets would be largely inconceivable within conventional architectural circumstances. They tease out the potential within the dynamic and unsupervised conditions found only in the seemingly fragile realm of the informal. Ultimately, it is the successful capitalization of these dynamic conditions that determines the value of the informal asset.

Site: Manshiyat Naser and Mokattam Village

Along the northwestern foothills of Mokattam Mountain, just a few miles from the Cairo Citadel and the towering Mosque of Muhammad Ali, lies one of Cairo's most notorious informal settlements, Manshiyat Naser. The settlement's notoriety does not primarily stem from the typical slum-like conditions associated with informal architecture, such as unsafe structures, lack of infrastructure, abject poverty, poor health conditions, and high crime rates, but rather from the extraordinary entrepreneurial spirit of the local communities, who have thrived in the face of this adversity.

This ingenuity is evidenced by such architectural achievements as the Cave Monastery of Saint Simon (Anba Samaan El-Kharraz), which was built, beginning in 1976, by carving deep into the limestone of Mokattam Mountain (Fig. 3.6). With the help and labor of the majority-Coptic population living in this area, the church stands today not only as a unique example of the collective resolve of a disenfranchised people to effectively self-organize but also a truly remarkable architectural feat that has incorporated topographical and material constraints into a marvelous cultural expression. Cultural expressions in Manshiyat Naser, however, are not limited to individual edifices in the vein of Saint Simon. As remarkable as these structures are, the phenomenon of the Zabbaleen may be even more impressive.

At the southern tip of Manshiyat Naser, nestled into the Mokattam hills, lies Mokattam Village, the infamous home and workplace of the garbage collectors.[67] The Zabbaleen have transformed this neighborhood into a fully functional trash recycling facility. In order to support the ecology of trash collection, sorting, and recycling, the streets and buildings here have multiple roles, attempting to balance the precarious demands of these processes with the residents' desire and need for safe and sanitary housing conditions. The informal nature of the buildings, with their unfinished and improvisational character, plays a crucial role in this endeavor

Fig. 3.6 Cave Monastery of Saint Simon, Mokattam Mountain, Cairo, 2016. (Photograph courtesy Ferda Kolatan.)

This remarkable church was carved into the limestone rock of Mokattam Mountain through the collaborative efforts of the Manshiyat Naser community. The rough texture of the carved rock has been ingenuously incorporated into the design and enhanced by intricate figures and reliefs.

by providing flexibility and adaptive physical properties that formal architecture would not allow.

If Saint Simon illustrates the capacity to address cultural (i.e., religious) needs amidst the dire and challenging conditions in informal settlements, the Zabbaleen demonstrate how an entire economy can be developed through peer-to-peer interactions. Nearly every structure in Manshiyat Naser, in some shape or form, embodies the vast and intricate convergence of disparate needs within this tightly packed urban conglomerate. These structures represent more than mere makeshift solutions; they are innovative architectural works with a unique aesthetic that undeniably qualifies them as legitimate cultural expressions.

NOTES

65 This is not to suggest that all real estate value is exclusively dependent on branding. But as evidenced by the brochures and fliers filling mailboxes and covering the windows of real estate agencies in coveted markets, "assets" are increasingly defined by a rather reductive and homogenous set of criteria.

66 The most well known among these satellite cities is New Cairo City, which was established in 2000 and has a population of over 1.5 million. Many smaller gated communities are being built along Cairo's major freeways and are advertised on large billboards lining the roadside. Cairo's population growth requires the expansion of its boundaries, but the satellite cities are environmentally harder to sustain and accelerate the impoverishment of the historical and cultural centers of the city.

67 A lot of information about the Zabbaleen is available online in books, news articles, and documentary films. An excellent source to delve deeper into the Zabbaleen community and the history of Mokattam Village is the writings and lectures of Dr. Laila Iskandar, who formerly headed the Ministry of State for Urban Renewal and Informal Settlements and Egypt's environment affairs ministry. For a brief summary of the topic, see: Laila Iskandar and Jens Chr. Tjell, "Cairo: A colossal case of waste mismanagement to learn from," *Waste Management & Research*, December 2009, https://journals. sagepub.com/doi/10.1177/0734242X09354030.

Figs. 3.7, 3.8 Informal settlement, Manshiyat Naser, Cairo, 2016. (Photograph courtesy Ferda Kolatan.)

The informal settlement is partially situated along the precarious edge of a cliff that is susceptible to landslides. The buildings typically range from two to six stories in height, supported by a concrete framework and enclosed by brick fill-in walls. Nearly all of these structures are in a raw and unfinished state. In Mokattam Village, the Zabbaleen have adapted the streets and buildings to facilitate their garbage collection and recycling endeavors. Trash collected from all over Cairo is brought here, meticulously sorted, and recycled in the apartment buildings before being sold to intermediaries.

The Belvedere

Unfinished structures account for the majority of buildings in Manshiyat Naser. This phenomenon can be attributed to two primary factors. The first is a general scarcity of adequate financial resources, which often results in disruptions and stoppages in the workflow during the construction phase. The second factor is the imperative for the structure to provide flexibility for its inhabitants. Leaving buildings unfinished enables them to more easily incorporate changes, such as additions, modifications, and expansions, to accommodate the evolving needs of a growing family. Consequently, these unfinished houses embody the dynamic living conditions that characterize the neighborhood. However, to outsiders or visitors, the "unfinished" state of these structures may be perceived as a serious flaw, instantly activating the stigma of poverty and decay.

The Belvedere transforms this perceived deficit into an asset by embracing a common design feature of informal architecture, in which the primary structure of the building remains partially exposed at both the bottom and the top. The absence of an enclosure on the ground floor allows for a more versatile usage, including work-related functions like small-scale manufacturing, sorting, and storing, and maintains a connection to the communal activities happening at street level. The enclosed intermediate floors serve as the main living quarters and are generally well-laid-out spaces with nice furnishings. The topmost floor functions as an interim open terrace, which can be used for maintaining pigeon lofts and other popular pastimes. In the event that additional floors are needed, they can be added without altering the organizational structure of the building.

Born of necessity, these structures are rather ingenious and reflect the needs and desires of their inhabitants, as well as the tools and materials they have access to. Their incompleteness invites an interesting comparison once it is no longer preconceived as a deficiency. The raised effect achieved by the enclosed midsection of the house, the piloti-like piers or columns arranged in a grid on the ground floor, the largely unobstructed and undivided entrance floor, and the roof terrace evoke the functionalist aesthetic of classical modernist villas from the early 20th century. These characteristics resonate particularly with Le Corbusier's five points defining the central characteristics of modern architecture: open floor plans, flexibility in layout, cubic geometries, free-flowing circulation, and the obligatory roof terrace.

The Belvedere harnesses the unfinished state of the buildings in Manshiyat Naser to forge a distinctive residential type alluding to the modernist villa. Positioned on an elevated plinth, the building's open entrance provides both privacy and separation from the street, while also serving as a robust foundation for its structural columns. Located at the center of the plinth, a staircase seamlessly connects the intermediate floors, which house the living and dining areas, kitchen, bedrooms, and bathrooms. The staircase extends all the way to the open roof terrace, which is safeguarded by a parapet that can be vertically expanded to accommodate additional floors if the need should arise in the future.

Informal Assets Catalogue

Fig. 3.9 Dunbee Choi & Joseph Giampietro, The Belvedere, rendering,
Cairo Studio, University of Pennsylvania Weitzman School of Design, 2016.

The Veiled Villa

In informal settlements it is common to see buildings that are either entirely or partially covered by large pieces of tarp or fabric. This practice safeguards the interiors of unfinished structures from the adverse effects of the region's challenging weather conditions: intense sunlight and erosive winds. Located on the fringes of the Sahara Desert, Cairo experiences predominantly cloudless skies for approximately 350 days a year. From April to October, daytime temperatures easily soar beyond 80 degrees Fahrenheit, reaching even higher levels during the peak summer months. The average breeze carries particles of fine sand, resulting in the material's deposition on all surfaces, leaving a delicate layer of yellow dust across the city.

Residents of informal settlements use tarp to mitigate the constant influx of sand into their living quarters, as well as to combat extreme heat. It is even frequently used in buildings with fully enclosed and air-conditioned rooms. The tarp covering creates a unique interstitial space that is defined by the elasticity of the tarp and its supple nature as a wrapping material. At times, the wrapper is tightly fastened to a surface, while at others, it is propped up to allow for access underneath. Inhabitants make use of these protected spaces for a variety of activities, including the small-scale manufacturing of household items, recycling, socializing, resting, and playing games.

Undeniably, the tarp assumes a crucial role in these contexts, serving as a legitimate building material that harnesses its advantageous properties: lightweight, affordable, flexible, breathable, and easy to install and manipulate. However, there is a prevailing perception that tarp is a secondary material, deemed unsuitable for integration into a more cohesive and durable building design. The presence of visible tarp on buildings often immediately denotes a site under construction or represents improvised solutions born of limited resources, economic hardship, and poverty. The Veiled Villa challenges this bias by incorporating tarp as a functional component that complements the solid construction elements of the building with a more malleable one, as well as by embracing it as an aesthetic feature.

The concept of the veil has a rich tradition in Islamic architecture, often associated with the intricate window tracery that protected views from the street level, enabling women to observe the outside while shielding them from the male gaze. However, the veil can be interpreted beyond its gendered origins, serving as an architectural device that playfully hints at forms without fully revealing them. The Veiled Villa, deeply rooted in the aesthetic language of informal settlements, explores the layered experience achieved by enveloping large urban objects, reminiscent of the work of artists Christo and Jean-Claude. Through its wrapping, the building's architectural elements become rounded and softened, seamlessly integrated under the fabric, while the facade gains new kinetic qualities as it responds to the movement of wind.

Informal Assets Catalogue

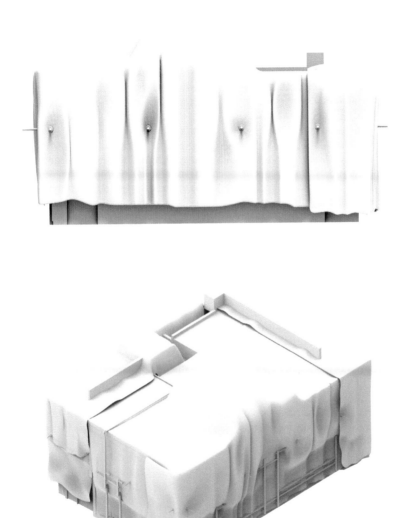

Fig. 3.10 Dunbee Choi & Joseph Giampietro, The Veiled Villa, rendering,
Cairo Studio, University of Pennsylvania Weitzman School of Design, 2016.

The Rock

Many buildings in the vicinity of Manshiyat Naser's Mokkatam Mountain are perched precariously on the edges of unstable limestone cliffs marked by menacing voids and cavities. These cliffs are prone to intermittent collapse, often leading to catastrophic landslides. In these unfortunate incidents, entire buildings are ruthlessly swept away as the slopes yield, resulting in serious injury and, tragically, even fatalities among the residents. Structures at the base of these inclines are often completely engulfed by the loose soil and debris cascading from the rocky precipices, exacerbating the devastation. Due to the scarcity of modern tools and financial support, the accumulation of debris becomes an insurmountable challenge for residents, who are unable to properly clean their homes and remove debris.

Constructing any building on the sandy and unstable terrain of Mokkatam, or anywhere in its immediate vicinity, is highly problematic and inadvisable due to the inherent risks involved. However, the residents of Mokkatam have no choice but to confront these hazardous circumstances. Instead of abandoning houses that have been damaged and partially buried under earth and rock, they adapt and repurpose them to the best of their abilities. The resulting architecture is a peculiar amalgamation of rock and building, born of adversity, and yet a testament to the resilient spirit, resourcefulness, and unwavering determination of the local communities.

The Rock exemplifies the locals' adaptive approach to the calamitous conditions in Mokkatam. Doors and windows irretrievably covered by fallen rock and earth are left that way, and the circulation of the house is reconfigured based on what is still accessible. Infrastructural elements such as downpipes and electrical circuits are also rerouted around the landslides. New windows and doors are carved roughly into the rock, forging a strange harmony between the house and its environment. The surrounding landscape is skillfully reshaped: smaller debris is used to create cement for filling gaps and stabilizing larger rock fragments. Furthermore, the total engulfment of the building by the landslide creates a communal rooftop. Accessible directly from the plateau of the cliff, the rooftop introduces a new vertical circulation throughout the house, allowing it to remain functional in the event that the lower-level entrances become blocked.

These modifications not only ensure the ongoing usability of the house but also imbue it with other unforeseen qualities. Through its hybridization with the rock, the building establishes a new and distinct sectional relationship with the landscape's topography. Rather than standing independently on the ground as it did in its original form, the rock house is now partially integrated into the slope. This transformation not only introduces novel possibilities for the internal arrangement of the building but also evokes intriguing formal and aesthetic resemblances to ancient rock dwellings, as well as to modern architectural masterpieces, Adalberto Libera's iconic Casa Malaparte in particular.

Informal Assets Catalogue

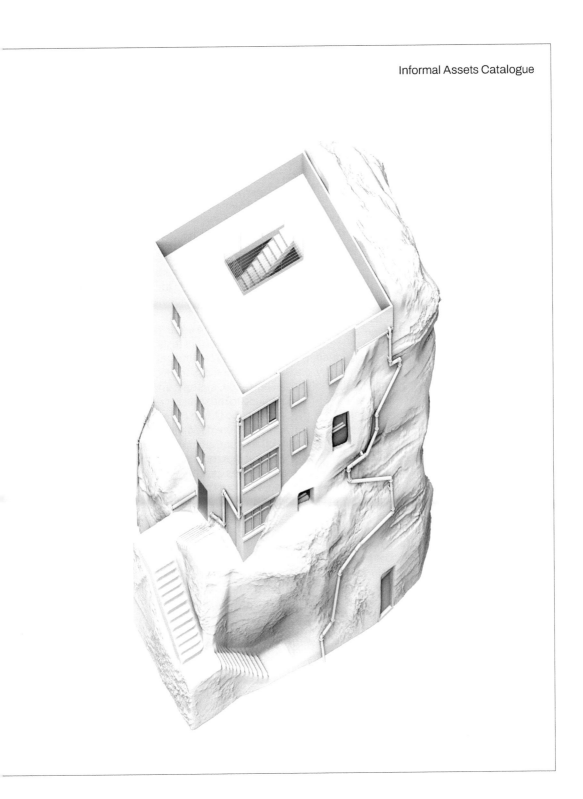

Fig. 3.11 Grace Kim & Rachel Lee, The Rock, rendering,
Cairo Studio, University of Pennsylvania Weitzman School of Design, 2016.

Urban Barn

Many buildings in Manshiyat Naser house animals. Donkeys, goats, sheep, chickens, geese, rabbits, and pigeons are among the most common nonhuman inhabitants. Across Cairo's settlement's, wooden pigeon lofts protrude from the rooftops. Pigeon breeding has a long-standing tradition in Egypt and remains popular to this day. These pigeons are used as messengers, kept as pets, used for racing, and valued as a culinary delicacy. In some cases, entire buildings once inhabited by humans are dedicated exclusively to animal sheltering and breeding, effectively becoming vertical farms.

The practice of keeping animals in close proximity to human quarters is driven by necessity, convenience, and practicality. Given the high prices of meat and dairy products, the rearing of livestock and poultry at home is more economically viable. Animals also serve as a form of currency for bartering and exchanging goods within the community. Due to the scarcity of outdoor spaces suitable for animal sheltering in informal settlements, residents' only option is often to keep these animals in their homes. This arrangement also simplifies the rearing of the animals, as they are fed with leftover food from the households.

The Urban Barn capitalizes on this hybrid concept, appropriating a seven-story structure to showcase the cohabitation of humans and animals in an informal urban setting. Existing wooden lifts and cranes, built to transport food and waste along the apartment facades, are replicated and transformed into a new kind of building envelope. Mounted along the roof parapets and the balcony edges, a simple and easy-to-operate pulley system hauls up fodder and brings down dung in return. This system also provides adjustable shading for the facade's many balconies and terraces, while giving the building a unique and intriguing semitransparent, tracery-like aesthetic that characterizes the informal construction methods used on site.

Although largely abandoned in modern times, in recent years there has been a notable resurgence in the age-old concepts of cohabitation between animals and humans. The reintegration of livestock into the urban realm has become an important testing ground for progressive ideas aimed at reducing the carbon footprint associated with food transportation, storage, and distribution. In addition to these larger environmental concerns, the Urban Barn also reduces waste in a more direct manner, as its inhabitants use animals only for their immediate personal needs, recycle food leftovers as fodder, and repurpose manure as fertilizer in small gardens and containers located throughout the building and the neighborhood.

Informal Assets Catalogue

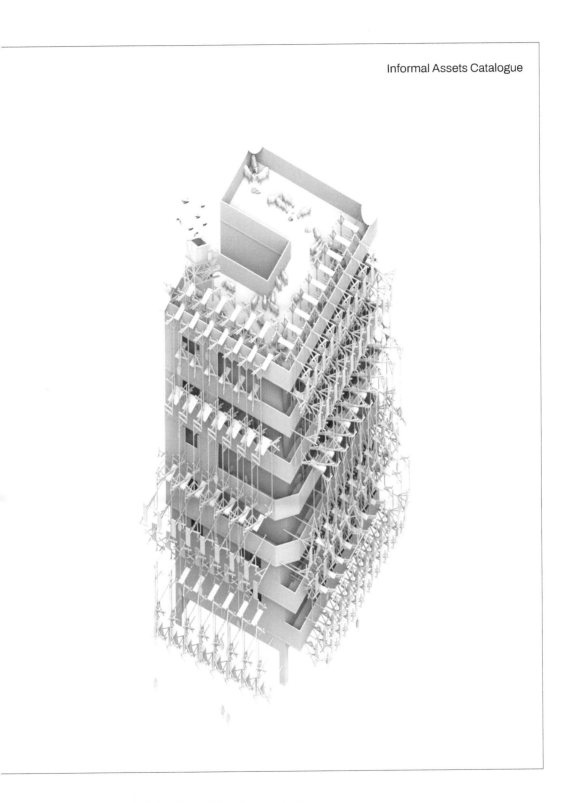

Fig. 3.12 Heng Gu & Chi Zhang, Urban Barn, rendering,
Cairo Studio, University of Pennsylvania Weitzman School of Design, 2016.

The Conjoined Mansion

Yet another intriguing phenomenon has emerged in Manshiyat Naser, in which new kinds of relationships are forged across multiple adjacent buildings through unexpected horizontal linkages. These architectural connections have developed organically in response to the evolving needs of expanding families and family relations. Two, and at times even three, separate buildings are cleverly joined together through the implementation of ad hoc ramps and bridges, as well as extensions to balconies and terraces that span the void between buildings.

This innovative approach to horizontal connectivity showcases resourcefulness and efficiency. One application of this practice involves the combination of rooms from neighboring buildings to form fully functional small apartment units, particularly suitable for newlyweds. When space in their current residence becomes limited, families can expand sideways into the adjoining building, all while maintaining a single entrance and circulation through their apartment.

This symbiotic relationship between buildings showcases the creative resourcefulness of the residents in tackling the practical challenges inherent to living in informal settlements. By embracing the concept of connectivity, these buildings surpass their individual boundaries, and create many opportunities for customization and expansion. These adaptations are facilitated by the unfinished nature of the structures and the absence of basic regulations that would typically prohibit the construction of buildings in such

close proximity to one another. While it is crucial to acknowledge that the addition of improvised elements such as temporary bridges or ramps without professional consultation can pose genuine safety hazards, it is important to bear in mind that all informal architecture is inherently "unregulated" and thus operates outside the requirements and restrictions of building codes and safety protocols.

The Conjoined Mansion merges two seven-story apartment buildings into a single spacious "superblock." The two structures are connected by a seamless system of ramps and terraces. While maintaining the design and functionality of the apartments, the terraces serve as malleable expansion zones, and express the changing family dynamics through new architectural configurations. The introduction of the ramps and walkways enhances and reinforces the existing makeshift crossings, ensuring improved safety and usability. Additionally, these outdoor connections create alternative pathways throughout the complex, which serve as discrete accessways to the private living quarters. The Conjoined Mansion assumes a distinctive, bridge-like appearance and provides a shaded open area beneath for communal recreational use.

Informal Assets Catalogue

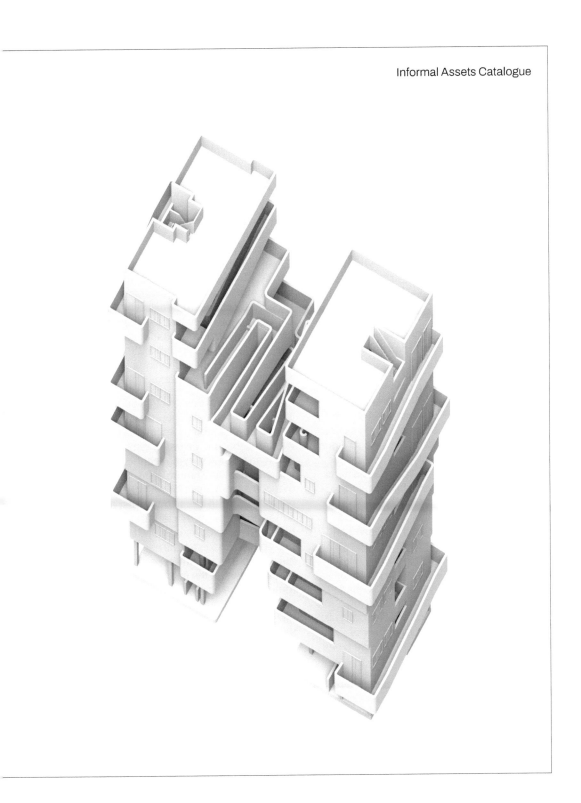

Fig. 3.13 Hyemi Kang & Brett Lee, the Conjoined Mansion, rendering,
Cairo Studio, University of Pennsylvania Weitzman School of Design, 2016.

The Loft

The rapid unregulated growth in Manshiyat Naser has generated an organic and rather opportunistic urban layout. The meandering streets are lined with buildings, most of which are in various states of decay or incompleteness. While typically creating an impression of disorder and perplexity for foreign visitors, the neighborhood's residents navigate this density with ease and efficiency. This labyrinthine streetscape manifests the various bottom-up architectural decision-making processes that are unique to the site and emerge from the interplay of available lots, their diverse shapes and sizes, and the mutual dependencies of neighborly relations.

While the majority of buildings in Manshiyat Naser follow a generally square layout, the absence of a predetermined organizational grid gives rise to shifts and deviations from one structure to another. These deviations produce all kinds of unexpected juxtapositions, gaps, and misalignments, resulting in oddly shaped spatial remnants and many triangular parcels of land. These parcels are often built over and incorporated into adjacent buildings in order to expand their usable interior space. Emerging from this practice are buildings with unorthodox shapes, larger floor plans, and distinctively oblique facades, all of which distinguish them from the more conventional square-plan units that otherwise typify informal housing.

The Loft is one such example, where the leftover parcels between two existing buildings are enclosed to create additional interior space, resulting in an atyp-ically elongated and angular building shape. These elongations involve deeper floorplans with more challenging circulatory routes to connect the building's once autonomous parts in newly functional ways. Drawing inspiration from industrial loft conversions, which have become trendy and sought-after real estate assets in many postindustrial cities worldwide, The Loft offers versatile warehouse-style interiors that can accommodate a multitude of programmatic hybridizations within a single expansive space. From residential units to office spaces, small-scale manufacturing facilities, and recreational areas, the open layout of The Loft fosters a range of possibilities for unique and creative programmatic combinations.

The architectural design of The Loft is anchored by robust concrete frames and complemented by adaptable brick-wall infills that can be easily removed or modified to meet varying requirements for ventilation and natural light. To overcome the accessibility challenges presented by the deep floor plans, a series of internal and external staircases have been added, linking different levels, and connecting disparate sections of the building that would otherwise be difficult to reach through the existing circulation routes. These strategically positioned stair units, although seemingly odd in their placement, become a distinctive aesthetic marker of the building and further enhance its likeness to the industrial warehouses that have evolved over time in response to new urban needs.

Informal Assets Catalogue

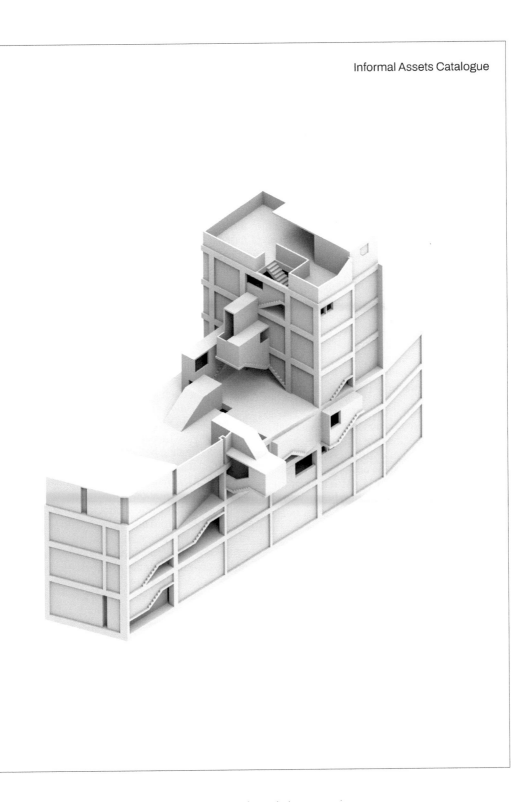

Fig. 3.14 Fan Cao & Hadeel Mohammad, The Loft, rendering,
Cairo Studio, University of Pennsylvania Weitzman School of Design, 2016.

The Conveyor House

Mokattam Village is distinct from most other informal settlements of Manshiyat Naser. As the home to the Zabbaleen, the renowned garbage collectors of Cairo, this neighborhood also operates as a large, distributed waste-collection and recycling facility. Along the narrow meandering streets and inside the seemingly run-down apartment buildings, the Zabbaleen have established an efficient system for sorting the city's garbage. Their system is so effective, in fact, that the percentage of reclaimed material from waste surpasses those of state-of-the-art industrial recycling plants. This remarkable achievement, like other productive endeavors in Manshiyat Naser, stems from the Zabbaleen's astute utilization of the limited resources available to them.

Nearly every corner of Mokattam Village has been transformed into an essential component of the recycling process. Through the concerted efforts of the community, waste is collected from all parts of Cairo and brought to Mokattam Village using small pick-up trucks and donkey carts. Once the garbage arrives, it is deposited in front of homes and diligently sorted by hand, taking into account material properties, use value, and the overall condition of the discarded items. To facilitate the sorting process, different piles representing distinct categories of materials are created. Recovered materials and objects are then allocated to the appropriate bins, containers, and large bags, ready to be sold to middlemen. Certain recovered materials are "upcycled" directly within the community, where skilled artisans repurpose them into handbags, totes, towels, drapes, toys, and other similar products, which are then sold in small stores around the neighborhood.

The Conveyor House is conceived as an upgraded component for this urban recycling facility, designed to accommodate the existing work and living routines of the Zabbaleen. Buildings are retrofitted with a simple conveyor belt system that capitalizes on the irregularities of informal structures. Overhangs, nooks, cavities, terraces, and other unenclosed areas of the buildings are repurposed to serve the recycling process, effectively separating work areas from the living quarters. This separation helps minimize the negative effects of noise, dust, and toxic off-gassing on the inhabitants.

The flexibility of the conveyor system allows for a unique approach to each existing building and can be extended to incorporate neighboring structures if necessary. The current practice of manually hauling heavy bags down from trucks and up several floors, often performed by children, is made obsolete by the implementation of the moving belt. A small backyard compost garden is established from the organic residue of the recycling process. Over time, the establishment of multiple Conveyor Houses creates a nodal system that concentrates all trash-related activities in a few areas within the neighborhood. The increased productivity of the machine-house hybrids frees up other areas in the community to develop without the burdensome effects of trash collection. Importantly, however, these developments do not impede the Zabbaleen's capacity for self-governance or hinder their ability to continue their business.

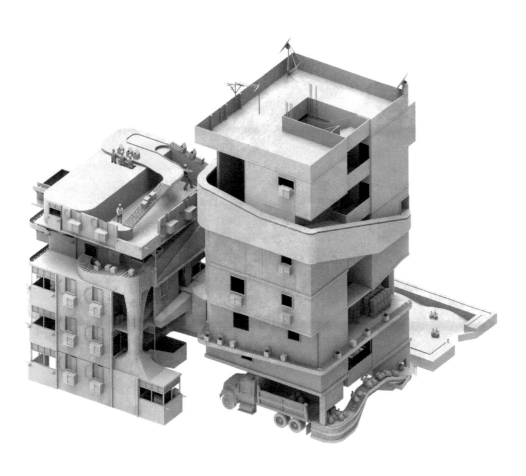

Fig. 3.15 Heng Gu & Chi Zhang, The Conveyor House, rendering,
Cairo Studio, University of Pennsylvania Weitzman School of Design, 2016.

The Ring Road

Site: Ezbet Khairallah

When viewed from above, the Ezbet Khairallah district in Cairo showcases one of its most distinct and impactful features: the presence of a highway that cuts through its core, effectively dividing the neighborhood in two. The construction of this partially elevated highway, known as the Ring Road, commenced in the late 1980s with the primary objectives of encircling the greater Cairo region, alleviating severe traffic congestion, and mitigating the encroachment of urban development on arable lands.[68] However, those responsible for the planning and implementation of the multilane Ring Road exhibited a stark lack of consideration for the communities it would directly impact, particularly with regard to districts characterized by a significant presence of informal structures such as Ezbet Khairallah.

From the municipality's perspective, these informal settlements are illegal, unsafe, dysfunctional, and unattractive. Consequently, the typical approach toward these neighborhoods is one of deliberate neglect, justified by the notion that their accelerated deterioration will eventually necessitate their wholesale demolition. There is rarely any consideration given to more sensible incremental approaches to legalize, repair, renovate, or if necessary, replace these informal buildings. In this context, the Ring Road, beyond its officially stated goals, further exacerbates and intensifies the urban isolation and socioeconomic impoverishment experienced by the Ezbet Khairallah communities.

The devastating effects of the Ring Road on the communities it bisects are made strikingly evident by its imposing presence as a colossal and intrusive barrier. Extending for miles and reaching a height of up to four meters, it has effectively severed in two what was once a tightly knit neighborhood, disrupting the intricate urban tapestry that had grown organically over decades. The consequences of this disruption manifest in abrupt spatial collisions, odd discontinuities, and other

Fig. 3.16 Aerial view of Ezbet Khairallah, Cairo, 2016. (Photograph courtesy Google Maps.)

This image reveals the expanse of the Ring Road highway and visualizes the scale of its impact on the urban fabric of Ezbet Khairallah.

Figs. 3.17, 3.18 The Ring Road, Ezbet Khairallah, Cairo, 2016.
(Photograph courtesy Rachel Lee)

Fig. 3.17: In between the highway wall and the adjacent buildings lies a continuous narrow strip of land. This inhospitable zone is filled with abandoned cars, litter, and other discarded objects. Fig. 3.18: Local artisans and vendors have appropriated this zone to advertise and sell their decorative plaster artifacts. The wall itself serves as a display, addressing potential customers on the highway and the streets below.

jarring architectural contradictions. One of the primary contributors to these dissonant urban moments is the road's concrete walls that slice perpendicularly across streets, buildings, and infrastructure. These walls, erected on both sides of the elevated highway to conceal its structural pillars, have come to symbolize the disregard and indifference exhibited by governmental planning agencies towards informal settlements and the communities they support.

By indiscriminately piercing through the densely populated areas of Ezbet Khairallah, the highway disrupts the essential commercial and practical connections necessary for the proper functioning of the neighborhood. The road also fractures deeply rooted and long-established familial and community ties that are vital for the social well-being of the neighborhood's residents. Yet, another consequence of the highway is the narrow and virtually unusable strip of land sandwiched between its sidewalls and the adjacent buildings. This confined space, along with the dead-end streets formed by the barrier, has become a desolate zone marred by litter, abandoned vehicles, and other discarded items. However, amidst this desolation, glimpses of resilience and creative adaptation by the locals emerge as they find ways to integrate these challenging conditions into their daily lives. Such interventions turn obstacles into assets.

The Decorated Wall

While navigating the narrow streets of Ezbet Khairallah in Cairo, one inevitably confronts the large concrete wall that seemingly appears out of nowhere. Lining both sides of the elevated Ring Road, this wall is a formidable obstacle, stretching for miles in either direction and interrupting the organic flow of the streets. In an effort to reestablish the vital commercial, practical, and social connections severed by the highway, the residents in this area have created strategic breaches by digging holes into the wall and building tunnel-like corridors to the opposite side. To illuminate these passages, electrical lines originally intended for lighting the highway have been cleverly tapped into. Outlets have been installed on the wall's surface, providing power for the tools and equipment used by the many laborers and craftspeople who call this area home. Even plumbing pipes have been diverted, ensuring a steady supply of water to the wall for the production of decorative plaster artifacts, a popular trade in the region.

These interventions have sparked an unforeseen reconfiguration of both the highway wall and the narrow space in front of it. Along this slender strip of land, a hybrid zone has emerged, facilitating various small-scale social, artisanal, and commercial activities, with the wall itself assuming the unlikely role of protagonist. Enterprising street vendors capitalize on the wall's presence by using it as a platform to showcase their plaster artifacts, including columns, ceiling rosettes, intricate moldings, and other decorative items. To capture the attention of passing drivers on the highway, the vendors strategically position these artifacts on the upper ledge of the wall. They also affix them directly onto the wall's surfaces to entice customers at the street level. Just behind the wall, one can find modest ateliers, storage depots, and utility kiosks that cater to the artisans crafting these artifacts.

The Decorated Wall embodies a captivating fusion between infrastructure and architecture, blurring the boundaries between obstacle and opportunity. Through the cumulative efforts of the residents to overcome its negative effects, the wall is transformed into a hybrid that integrates disparate elements, materials, and scales into a new kind of urban architecture. The skillfully crafted plaster rosettes and decorative objects blend into the wall's rugged surface. But not all wall-objects are mounted for display purposes only. Some of these handcrafted items, such as sinks and fountains, are functional, providing operational amenities to the wall and the surrounding communities. Additional cables, pipes, and other practical hardware components also adorn the wall, weaving and intertwining across its surface like an alien form of ornament.

Ultimately, The Decorated Wall pays unlikely tribute to the entrepreneurial spirit and improvisational competence displayed by the people of Ezbet Khairallah. In the face of adversity, the formidable barrier of the Ring Road becomes the locus of small-scale innovations and ad hoc customizations. Achieved through simple means, these interventions directly address the needs of the local population and demonstrate their self-reliance and resourcefulness. Converted into a potentially miles-long canvas for showcasing artisanal and practical objects, the wall takes

Figs. 3.19, 3.20 Grace Kim & Rachel Lee, Decorated Wall, renderings, Cairo Studio, University of Pennsylvania Weitzman School of Design, 2016.

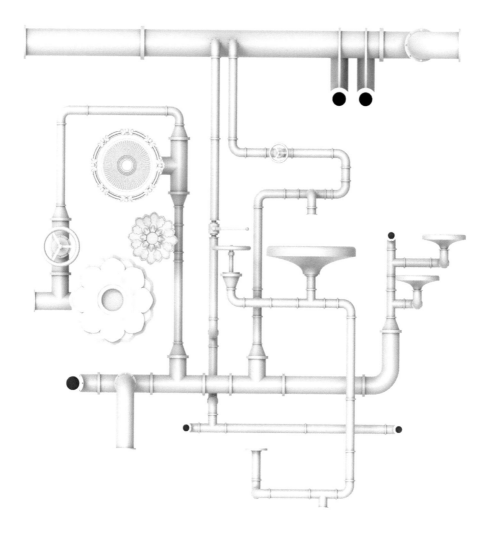

Figs. 3.21, 3.22 Above and opposite: Grace Kim & Rachel Lee, Hybrid Artifacts, renderings, Cairo Studio, University of Pennsylvania Weitzman School of Design, 2016.

on a strange aesthetic. It draws from the diverse qualities of the neighborhood, be they positive or negative, and creates an intriguing overlap of intentional and accidental influences.

The Highway's Underbelly

The Ring Road in Ezbet Khairallah not only splits the neighborhood into two separate zones but also creates a horizontal datum line, further dividing these zones into two distinct sections. Above the highway, the buildings are more or less unaltered. But below the highway, the apartment buildings and the surrounding public spaces face significant disadvantages. Confined within the narrow, trench-like corridors between the Ring Road's concrete wall and the lower portions of the adjacent buildings, these areas are desolate and unwelcoming, while offering no real opportunity for improvement. As discussed in the section above, one approach to this challenging zone is to concentrate on the wall itself and facilitate its transformation into a versatile hybrid object, tailored to suit the specific needs of the community.

In the same spirit, but with a particular emphasis on the neighborhood's horizontal division between upper and lower sections, The Highway's Underbelly employs an alternative strategy. The area below the highway is extended–spatially and conceptually–to include the corridor formed by the wall and the bottom floors of the adjacent buildings. The combined area is subsequently transformed into a compact and covered bazaar. To this end, a tented structure is erected that spans from the structural piers supporting the highway to the building facades opposite it. By covering a significant portion of this interstitial space, the tent creates a partially enclosed and shaded area that can provide for a cooler and more inviting environment, particularly during the hot summer months. Existing infrastructural elements, such as disorderly water and electrical lines strewn across the streets, highway walls, and building facades, are channeled through cavities within the tent structure to declutter the bazaar area and make it more functional.

The ground floors of the adjacent apartment buildings, previously isolated and devoid of views, natural light, and accessibility due to the presence of the highway, are reconfigured to establish a connection with the tented space. By linking the main staircases of the buildings to the covered bazaar, a direct pathway from the apartments to the market is established. These connections are designed to generate additional spaces that can be utilized by the locals as coffee shops or other storefronts, enhancing the cultural ambiance and functionality of the newly envisioned street market. This integration aims to revive the teeming public spaces that ruled these streets prior to the construction of the highway, and to nurture the social interactions that are essential to the overall atmosphere and vitality of the area.

Above the highway, the apartment buildings remain unaltered, except for the addition of new roof terraces. These terraces can be utilized privately or in conjunction with the cafes and shops at the street level and within the covered bazaar. The negative impact of the Ring Road on the neighborhood necessitates this

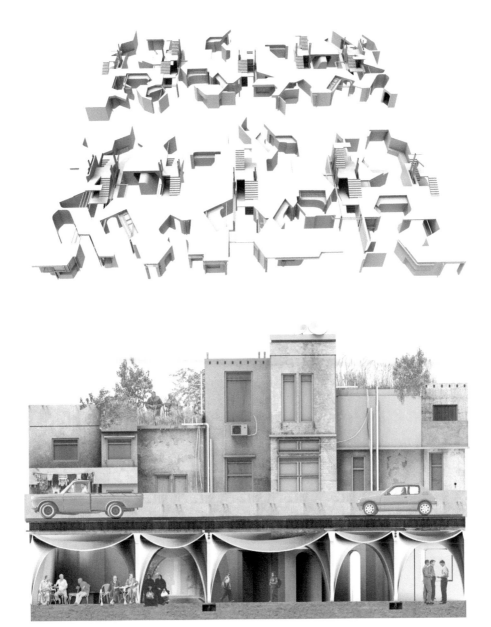

Figs. 3.23, 3.24 Yanghui Huang & Xinyue Zhang, Informal Assets, renderings, Cairo Studio, University of Pennsylvania Weitzman School of Design, 2016.

restructuring of the dysfunctional and inhospitable areas below and alongside the highway into an extended social and commercial zone where the public and private interests of the community meet.

The Gabkhana

Site: Istabl Antar

Adjacent to Ezbet Khairallah, just a little farther west along the Ring Road, is the district of Istabl Antar. Buried within this settlement lies the Gabkhana, a gun powder and ammunitions depot built in 1829 during the reign of Muhammad Ali Pasha. This former military complex in Old Cairo has long since been abandoned, closed off to the public, and left to deteriorate for decades. Recognizing its historical significance, the Egyptian government has recently designated the Gabkhana as a heritage site. Currently, efforts are underway to restore the facility and repurpose it as a cultural venue with the ultimate goal of breathing new life into the impoverished neighboring areas and enhancing their appeal to both tourists and residents alike.[69]

It is astonishing to consider that a structure like the Gabkhana complex exists within the densely populated, predominantly informal, and haphazardly developed neighborhood that surrounds it. Constructed when this area was mostly desert, the depot now stands as an isolated stronghold, resisting the encroaching city with its sturdy fortified walls. Inside the fort, there is a large courtyard spanning approximately 20,000 square meters, the tranquility of which sharply contrasts with the bustling streets just beyond its boundaries. The entrance to the courtyard is not easily located by pedestrians, as the city's irregular patterns of growth appear to have overlooked the existence of this historical structure.[70] Only through serendipity or with the assistance of locals does one stumble upon it. Encounters

Fig. 3.25 Aerial view of the Gabkhana heritage site in Istabl Antar, Cairo, 2016. (Photograph courtesy Google Maps.)

The ammunitions depot is located at the center of a fortified courtyard. The size and square shape of the armory, along with the pronounced presence of the nearby Ring Road, create a noticeable juxtaposition against the organic and small-scale structure of the surrounding urban fabric.

Fig. 3.26 Gabkhana, Istabl Antar, Cairo, 2016. (Photograph courtesy Ferda Kolatan)
The spaciousness and proportions of the courtyard impart a quality of seclusion and detachment upon the depot, effectively shielding it from the bustling communal life beyond its perimeter. In the contemporary context of Old Cairo and its surrounding informal settlements, the armory's lack of windows gives it a shrine-like aura, adding to its distinctive character.

with the courtyard are generally characterized by the sudden shift from the small-scale and unpredictable patchwork of the surrounding urban fabric to a serene clearing with the shrine-like depot at its center.

The depot measures approximately 30 by 95 meters with a height of 10 meters. It is supported by nine prominent piers along its longer sides and three on the shorter ends. The sturdy and substantial armory is primarily devoid of windows, except for a few embrasure-like openings. The building's facades have largely deteriorated, revealing varied material conditions beneath, including the underlying structural masonry and layers of discolored plaster applied over time. The partial separation of these layers has created an unconventional pattern that envelops the external walls of the depot, contributing to its distinctively weathered appearance.

The building's interior offers a somber and dim atmosphere, with limited light penetrating its narrow slits of window. The main space, where gunpowder barrels were once stored, is organized on a square grid and boasts a vaulted ceiling with forty shallow domes. The entrance area and auxiliary spaces have arches and barrel ceilings, further enhancing the disorienting effects of the depot's interior. This disorientation provides an intriguing contrast to the clear and orderly mass of the building's symmetrical exterior. Further complicating the legibility of the interior is a small basement that has been excavated beneath the main entrance floor. This basement does not adhere to the grid that organizes the rest of the building, adding to the complexity of its internal layout.

The Vault

The transformation of the Gabkhana from a solitary ammunitions depot in the desert into a tranquil urban enclave over the course of two centuries reflects not only the rapid expansion of Cairo into a megalopolis but also how the perceived significance of such monumental structures has changed over time. Once an imposing display of military might and state power, the fortified castle now assumes a concealed and shrine-like presence. It no longer asserts dominance from a distance but instead exudes a more intimate and enigmatic aura from within. This shift in how the Gabkhana is perceived is a constitutive factor for the Vault. Here, the armory is transformed into an urban sanctuary, a place for retreat and exploration that benefits the neighborhood without turning it into a landmark primarily geared toward attracting tourists.

The Vault asserts the value of seclusion in a neighborhood devoid of public spaces suitable for relaxation, introspection, and discovery. To maintain the complex's current level of visibility and accessibility, the fortification walls, courtyard, and courtyard entrance are left untouched, with the intervention focusing primarily on the interior. The existing arches, vaults, and domes inside the depot are taken as a formal/structural language from which new geometrical variations emerge via simple techniques of filleting, chamfering, extruding, and sweeping. The

Fig. 3.27 Fan Cao & Brett Lee, Gabkhana, section rendering, Cairo Studio, University of Pennsylvania Weitzman School of Design, 2016.

resulting geometries retain an affinity to the structural and spatial characteristics of the original architecture, while allowing for a reorganization of the labyrinthine interior into spaces conducive to hosting cultural events and more private and tranquil chambers, cavities, and poche spaces.

The exterior walls of the depot undergo slight modifications that reflect the changes within. The weathering and material delamination of the facades have created patterns out of the irregular edges of peeling layers of decaying plaster. By superimposing the outlines of the internal structural components onto these edges and reshaping the plaster layers to match, a new facade ornamentation emerges. This modified formal language, reflecting the cultural and tectonic features of the armory, seamlessly blends the residual material effects of the passage of time. Additionally, the shift from object of distant perception to one of intimate encounter that defines the Gabkhana is mirrored by the inversion of interior structural elements onto the facade.

The Vault celebrates the Gabkhana as a hidden monument, accentuating its unique history and site-specific themes of retreat and concealment. The material traces scarring the building, whether the deteriorating effects of the harsh desert climate or man-made, are considered as relevant components and are deliberately integrated into the treatment of the armory's facades. In terms of programming, The Vault deliberately maintains its flexible capacity to facilitate both planned and spontaneous activities and events. As such, the Gabkhana holds the potential to evolve into a thriving public space or, as the initial novelty fades, may eventually return to its secluded nature, as a cloistered reprieve from the bustling cityscape.

NOTES

68   Nezar Alsayyad, *Cairo: Histories of a City* (Cambridge: Harvard University Press, 2011), 263–64.

69   At the time of our visits to Cairo in 2016/'17, no specific plans had been publicly disclosed regarding a restoration of the heritage site. However, in 2022 the Egyptian Ministry of Tourism officially announced its intention to restore the Gabkhana as part of a comprehensive plan to revitalize Old Cairo and give a "facelift" to the surrounding informal areas. Ahmed Gomaa, "Egypt Launches Renovation of Rare Weapon Cache Dating Back to Muhammad Ali Pasha Era," *Al-Monitor*, May 2, 2022, https://www.al-monitor.com/originals/2022/04/egypt-launches-renovation-rare-weapon-cache-dating-back-muhammad-ali-pasha-era.

70   Recent aerial photographs from 2022 show a clearing of the residential areas to the west of the courtyard and new developments, including large sports facilities. The observations mentioned here refer to the time of our visit in 2016.

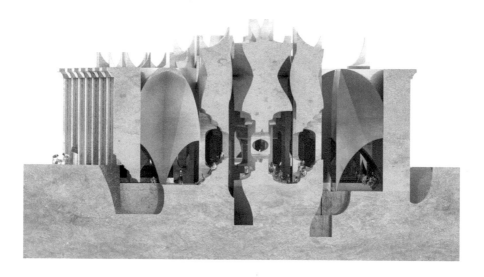

Figs. 3.28, 3.29, 3.30 Above and opposite: Fan Cao & Brett Lee, Gabkhana, renderings, Cairo Studio, University of Pennsylvania Weitzman School of Design, 2016.

Elevation, section, and interior view of the converted ammunitions depot.

Over/Under

Cairo's Bridges

Located right at the bifurcating tip of the Nile River delta, Cairo has depended on this mythical stream since ancient times. Serving as a lifeline from the Stone Age onward, the seasonal ebbs and floods of the mighty Nile created fertile lands, ensuring a steady supply of crops and giving rise to the great civilizations along its banks. In modern times, as the city expanded to include an increasingly larger portion of arable land, the Nile serves primarily industrial and transportation purposes. Today, several bridges span the river, connecting Cairo's eastern and western sides and linking the major traffic arteries that surround and crisscross the city.

While the overall challenge posed by Cairo's traffic is daunting and will require long-term planning and transition strategies to resolve, the bridges themselves also pose a more localized and immediate problem for the residents. As these bridges cut deeply into the shores, disrupting the adjacent urban fabric with massive overhangs, underpasses, and on- and off-ramps, creating dark, inhospitable, and chaotic intersections in the areas where these features meet the ground. These bridges were constructed to accommodate vehicular traffic, with little to no consideration of the needs and safety of the large number of pedestrians, who must use these landings and intersections to navigate the city. With the absence of adequate traffic signals, regulated crossings, or footbridges, pedestrians forced to navigate these obstacles must do so under often hair-raisingly perilous and impractical conditions.

By cutting into the coastal fabric, running perpendicular to the flow of the Nile, the bridges not only fracture the city into separate segments, but also impede access to the waterfront of the Nile Corniche, a continuous, multilane boulevard running alongside the river's banks. The Corniche serves as a major north-south traffic artery, while also providing space for much-needed leisure-oriented and recreational programs thanks to its adjacent pedestrian promenade. The revitalization of the Corniche, particularly in the downtown area, as a social and recreational zone has become a widely discussed topic in Cairo, leading to the implementation of government-sanctioned initiatives and projects.[71]

The projects featured in "Over/Under" are positioned within this dual context of municipal efforts to revitalize the Corniche and enhance the recreational and

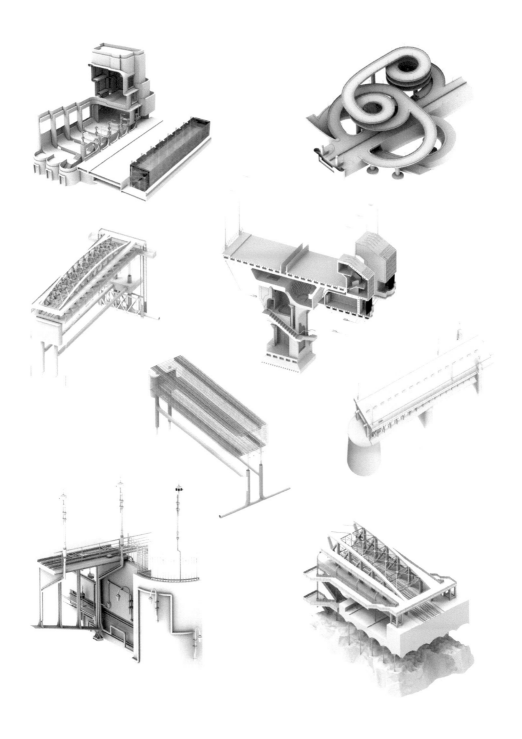

Fig. 3.31 Over/Under, study renderings,
Cairo Studio, University of Pennsylvania Weitzman School of Design, 2017.

Fig. 3.32 Aerial views of the bridge landing sites used for Over/Under, 2022. (Photograph courtesy Google Maps.)

From the left: East-bank landing of the 6th of October Bridge, east-bank landing of the Imbaba Bridge, Zamalek-landing of the Casr El Nil Bridge, and the west-bank landing of the Imbaba Bridge. These bridges all roughly connect to the Downtown Cairo area on the eastern bank, and/or Zamalek, a man-made island which once was a geographical part of the west bank. Zamalek is mostly populated with sports facilities, gardens, and clubs, with affluent residential areas in the northern part of the island.

commercial value of the adjacent downtown district and the challenging yet lively street conditions at the bridge landings. These projects are conceived as urban and infrastructural hybrids with a specific focus on the landing areas of three prominent bridges in the vicinity of downtown and Zamalek Island: The Imbaba Bridge (railway), the 6th of October Bridge, and the Casr El Nil Bridge. The current structural, infrastructural, and material properties of these sites are carefully modeled and presented as distinctive and desirable architectural elements. These models form the basis of the finalized architectural artifacts. Similar to "Informal Assets," this chapter concerns itself with the kinds of design features that are easily overlooked or disregarded as irrelevant or antithetical to serious efforts toward urban improvement.

As is the case with all hybrid artifacts displayed in this book, the following projects can be understood as individual local follies or as interlinked constituents of a comprehensive theme, aiming at the transformation of disorderly or disadvantaged urban areas into testing grounds for novel design ideas. The physical properties of the bridge landings are characterized by odd and uncoordinated juxtapositions and overlaps. Roads, ramps, underpasses, walls, stairs, trusses, cables, guardrails, light poles, electrical conduits, canals, and numerous other elements interlock in a constant and often ungainly embrace. However, instead of viewing these conditions as the passive results of happenstance, here they are recognized as active convergences that hold the key to design techniques based on the appropriation of existing structures.

Adhering to the principles outlined in this book, these bridge artifacts embrace a new aesthetic that draws inspiration from local material practices. Whether they are small, ad hoc, and intimate or on a larger scale, these practices are tweaked to create novel forms. In these forms, one can discover the programmatic and performative potential derived from the unique characteristics of the surrounding environment. The divisions in the urban fabric created by the bridge landings and the other obstacles they pose, particularly for pedestrians, are sometimes alleviated and at others transformed into unexpected encounters. These encounters are designed to appeal, provoke, and engage passersby. In contrast to the linear development along the Corniche, with its focus on providing a clear and program-matically legible leisure program, the bridge artifacts target hidden corners and solitary spaces embedded deep within the bridge structures.

"Over/Under" draws from precedents such as the medieval Ponte Vecchio in Florence, where the structural and programmatic properties of the bridge become extensions of a bustling city life. One can seamlessly traverse the bridge, moving along a consistent row of small stores, without registering the transition from the street. However, at certain points, inevitable glimpses of the Arno River appear between the shops, reminding us of the bridge's existence and our physical rela-tionship to it. This kind of ambiguity between various architectural and spatial conditions and the users' intermittent awareness of them is characterized by a subtle tension, which, at any given moment, can produce surprising, even thrilling, encounters in the city. The bridge artifacts are presented primarily as diptychs, juxtaposing object models with close-up views in order to highlight this tension.

NOTES

71 The "Promenade for Egypt's People" (PEP, Mamsha Ahl Masr) is one such project aimed at creating publicly accessible two-level promenades for residents and visitors that overlook the Nile and integrate its waterfront more successfully with the city. This project is part of a broader initiative to upgrade Cairo's downtown area and make it more attractive for businesses and tourism. For more details about this project, visit the official government website, www.sis.gov.eg or see: Dina Ezzat, "Reconnecting to the Nile," *Ahram Online*, November 13, 2020, https://english.ahram.org.eg/NewsContent/50/1208/393497/AlAhram-Weekly/Features/Reconnecting-to-the-Nile.aspx.

Fig. 3.33 Angela Huang & Alex Tahinos, Over/Under, rendering,
Cairo Studio, University of Pennsylvania Weitzman School of Design, 2017.

In this model of the Casr El Nil Bridge landing on Zamalek Island, the circular geometry of Opera Square is integrated into a new waterfront architecture with a promenade, terraces, restaurants, and other recreational amenities. Unused existing piers are transformed into community gardens.

Cairo

Figs. 3.34, 3.35 Above and opposite: Angela Huang & Alex Tahinos, Over/Under, renderings, Cairo Studio, University of Pennsylvania Weitzman School of Design, 2017.

This rendering shows a portion of the promenade architecture. Water from the Nile is filtered and used to irrigate new green areas, around which cafes and restaurants are organized. Hybridizations between water-intake valves and wall ornaments create unique aesthetic expressions.

186

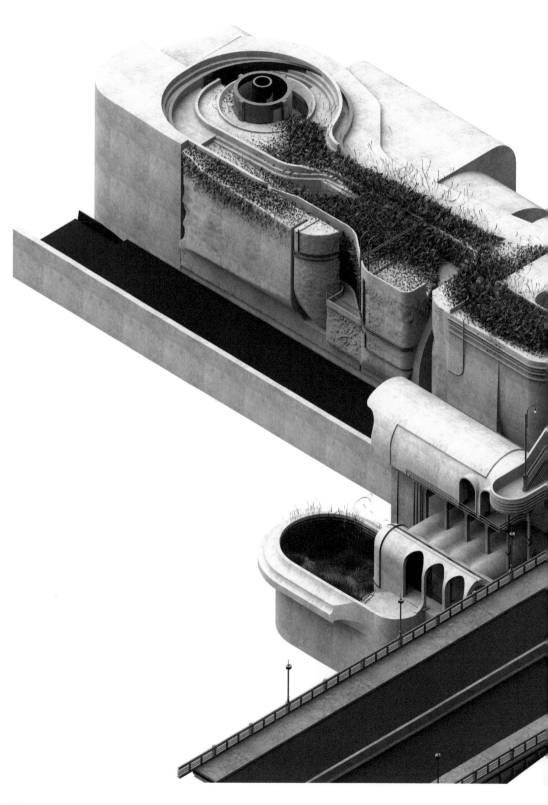

Fig. 3.36 Carrie Frattali & Angeliki Tzifa, Over/Under, rendering,
Cairo Studio, University of Pennsylvania Weitzman School of Design, 2017.

Another model depicting the Zamalek side of the Casr El Nil Bridge. The 19th-century
bronze lion statues guarding the bridge entrance signal staircases that take pedestrians
to the waterfront. A small water-treatment facility develops from the stairways, continuing
the curvilinear language of Opera Square.

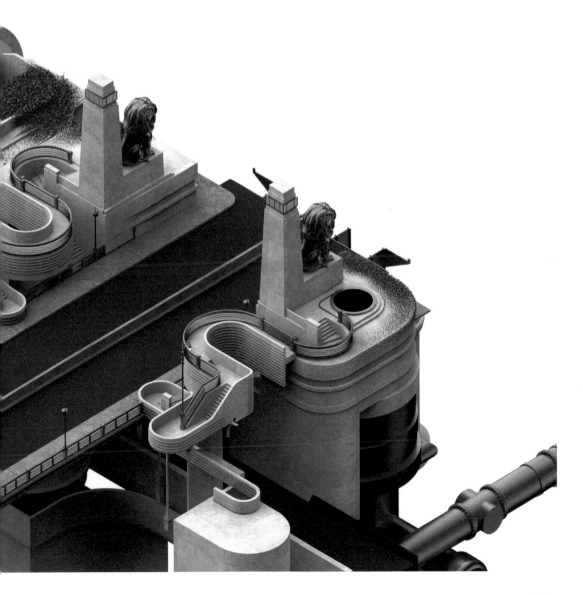

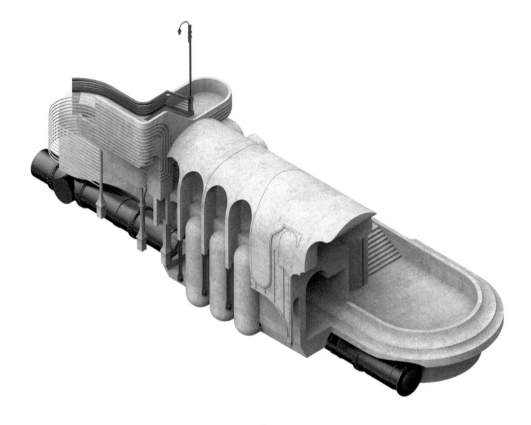

Figs. 3.37, 3.38 Above and opposite: Carrie Frattali & Angeliki Tzifa, Over/Under, rendering, Cairo Studio, University of Pennsylvania Weitzman School of Design, 2017.

Infrastructural, architectural, and decorative elements blend into new configurations.

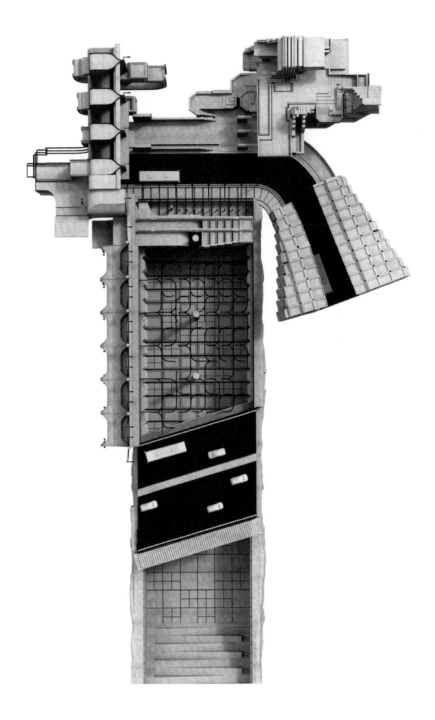

Figs. 3.39, 3.40 Above: Kyuhun Kim and Meari Kim. Opposite: Angeliki Mavroleon & Rosanna Pitarresi, Over/Under, renderings, Cairo Studio, University of Pennsylvania Weitzman School of Design, 2017.

With slight modifications to their roads and ramps, the landing areas of the Imbaba Bridge (Fig. 3.39) and the 6th of October Bridge (Fig. 3.40) reveal spatial pockets that can be utilized with new programs.

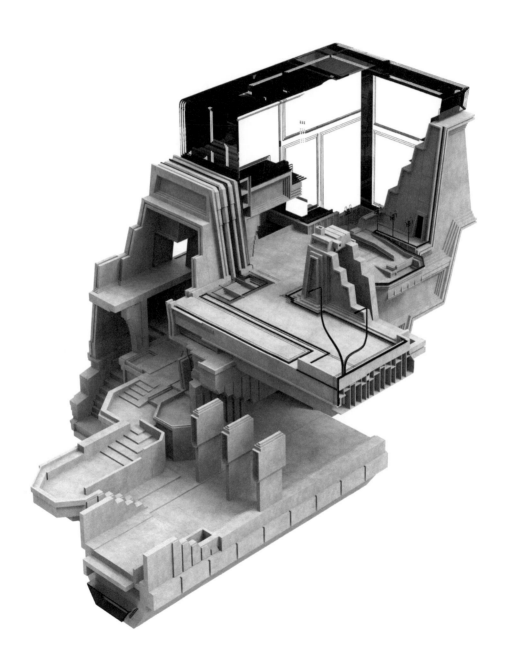

Figs. 3.41, 3.42 Above and opposite: Kyuhun Kim & Meari Kim, Over/Under, renderings, Cairo Studio, University of Pennsylvania Weitzman School of Design, 2017.

The complex section of the 6th of October Bridge landing is incorporated into a sculpted public plinth that serves as an entrance to a new office tower. The facades of the tower integrate photovoltaic panels, and the underpass cavities are repurposed into a sequence of event spaces.

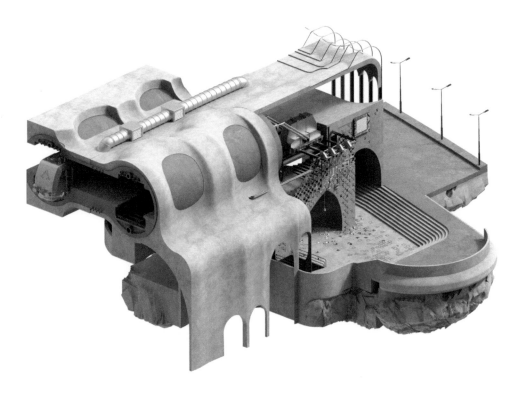

Figs. 3.43, 3.44 Above and opposite: Aly Abouzeid & John Darby, Over/Under, renderings, Cairo Studio, University of Pennsylvania Weitzman School of Design, 2017.

Section model of the Imbaba Railway Bridge with a new enclosure/facade (Fig. 3.43). The design enables pedestrians to pass underneath the elevated tracks and access small gathering areas beneath the vaulted staircase (Fig. 3.44).

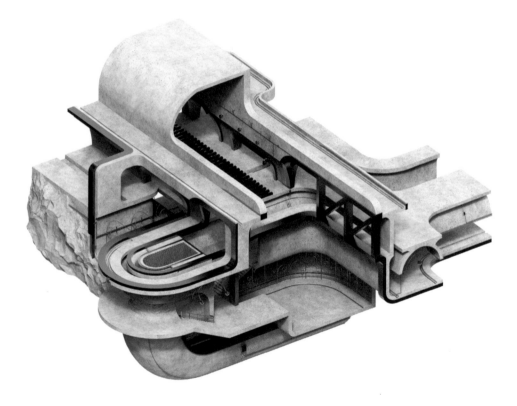

Figs. 3.45, 3.46, 3.47 Above, opposite, and next spread: Angeliki Mavroleon & Rosanna Pitarresi, Over/Under, renderings, Cairo Studio, University of Pennsylvania Weitzman School of Design, 2017.

Section model depicting the east-bank landing of the Imbaba Railway Bridge (Fig. 3.45). The formal and structural language of the bridge's tracks and trusses have been modified to create a series of interstitial chambers and corridors, facilitating new ways of crossing the bridge. The insides of these chambers provide room for local shops and feature walls adorned with peculiar ornaments made from cultural and utilitarian elements found on site (Figs. 3.46,3.47).

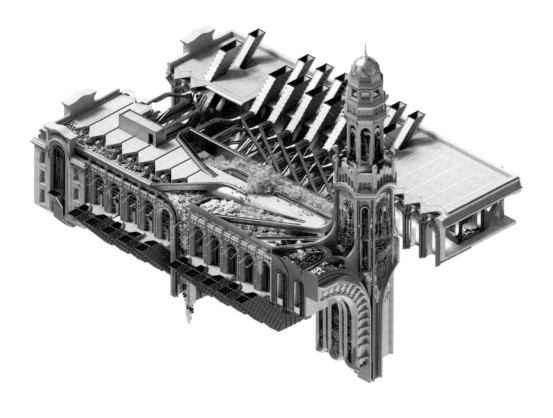

Fig. 4.1 Matt Kohman & Paul McCoy, Trinity Building, renderings,
New York Studio, University of Pennsylvania Weitzman School of Design, 2020.

New York

Authenticity Without Origin

More than any other metropolis, New York City, and in particular the island of Manhattan, has historically been associated with the ability to reinvent itself and take on new guises. Caught between old European heritages and traditions on the one hand, and the spirit of exploration driven by technological innovation and economic opportunities on the other, the city that concludes our trilogy has undergone numerous transformational shifts that have left their marks across its rich urban fabric.[72] One of these shifts, occurring between 1900 and the Great Depression, provides the source buildings for the hybrid artifacts in this section.

During this period, New York City saw its population double, from roughly three and a half million to almost seven million, and underwent unparalleled expansion fueled by advancements in steel construction, elevator technology, and more efficient mechanical systems.[73] Coupled with the city's rising status as the financial capital of the world, these developments ushered in the era of high-rises, bridges, and tunnels, turning Manhattan into the modern metropolitan powerhouse that it is today. In the words of the acclaimed filmmaker Fritz Lang, who was both awed and alarmed by the city's early 20th-century development: "I looked into the streets–the glaring lights and the tall buildings–and there I conceived *Metropolis*."[74]

Lang's utterance captures many of the tropes that have accompanied New York in the popular imagination throughout the 20th-century, establishing a lasting mythology for the city: a dynamic juggernaut that fearlessly embraces change as the essential harbinger of progress and prosperity, and a perpetual testing ground for radical urban and architectural experimentation and innovation. The plethora of utopian schemes–realized, unrealized, and totally fictional–devised for New York by leading planners, landscapers, engineers, and architects attest to this view and highlight the city's capacity to foster a uniquely creative cultural atmosphere in which speculative ideas, theoretical inquiries, and architectural narratives can thrive freely.[75]

Yet, the notion of Manhattan as the quintessential embodiment of the modern spirit is a somewhat misleading sentiment when it comes to its buildings. The early 20th century primarily produced its own kind of architectural misfit, characterized by the contradictory expressions of advanced structural, technical, and mechanical systems and the neoclassical and eclectic facades that concealed them.[76] This is the case for the gate and colonnades of the Manhattan Bridge and for the bank buildings and financial institutions that are the focus of the projects featured in the "Estranged Monuments" chapters. The grandiose facades, symmetrical proportions, and precious ornamentation of these structures once evoked a sense of authority, prestige, and familiarity in their reference to compositional elements of ancient temples, medieval cathedrals, and other revered building typologies. Moreover, these elements aimed to instill in the observer a sense of their authenticity, which couched the new within the familiar symbolic and formal language of a cherished European lineage.

Today, however, these buildings often appear adrift, devoid of authentic meaning–anachronistic apparitions hopelessly out of sync with the ceaseless dynamism and the diverse constituencies comprising the modern city. Their symbolism is illegible to most contemporary observers, overshadowed by the rapid and countless cycles of change and renewal that typify New York. All this sets the stage for the following projects, which employ techniques akin to the process of artification briefly touched on in the "Urban Misfits" chapter of this book. The loss of a reference to a spatio-temporal and cultural origin that characterizes the structures addressed in this section becomes the prerequisite for the emergence of new objects and practices that fill the void. New York's tendency to perpetually reinvent itself might break with existing traditions but, in turn, it also establishes a new kind of authenticity for its architecture.

Authenticity, as defined here, no longer relies on singular notions of an originary time, place, or tradition; instead, it derives from the combinatorial nature of the forms produced by this endless change. Understood in the context of hybrid artifacts, authenticity is thus not an inherent quality within things but rather a value produced through the convergence of external factors. In the words of Barbara Cueto and Bas Hendrikx: "Authenticity has become the ultimate asset. Originally, it was linked to the idea of a core of a thing–its essence. Recently, however, as a consequence of globalization and the ubiquity of technology, we are witnessing new ways of creating authenticity and processes of authentication that differ radically from this notion."[77] Defining authenticity not as a predetermined value but as intrinsically negotiable and contingent on context and change challenges inflexible worldviews based on categorical distinctions, and promotes a healthier design ecology rooted primarily in reuse and integration.

Perhaps no other work has expressed the playful, ambiguous, and aberrant nature of hybrids in such lasting and vivid form as Ovid's *Metamorphoses*.[78] In these infamous poems, gods, humans, animals, and plants shift shapes, dissolve, and recombine, giving rise to new unions, conjuring bizarre chimerical forms, and weaving new tales both instructive and captivating. Why should architectural components be an exception in this world of perpetual change? The adage "everything changes, nothing perishes" reminds us that origins are not static points fixed in time but fictional concepts around which we construct our value systems and worldviews. Change is but a rearrangement of existing matter. When seen from this perspective, objects do not simply materialize out of thin air through acts of creation, nor do they simply vanish once they no longer align with our interests. Instead, they persist, transform, and adapt, assuming different roles along the way.

NOTES

72   The region's urban history extends back roughly 15,000 years, to the first indigenous settlements in North America. The Lenape people lived in Manhattan (Manahatta) in small villages and practiced horticulture. Following the establishment of the colonial trading post New Amsterdam by the Dutch West India Company in 1624 and its subsequent conquest by the British in 1664, the Lenape were displaced from their ancestral lands. Only a few traces of Lenape settlements remain today, including the Bowery, which was once a Lenape trading route, and Astor Place, which served as an important powwow point.

73   U.S. Census Bureau, 1900–1930 – Fifteenth Census of the United States: 1930, Population, Volume 6, Families, Table 4.

74   The quote refers to Lang's 1927 dystopian masterpiece *Metropolis*. For generations, this film established New York as the epitome of the industrial megacity, being equal parts awe-inspiring, exhilarating, and frightening.

75   Among the realized schemes, one might think of the Manhattan Grid, Central Park, and the large infrastructural and urban renewal projects undertaken by Robert Moses. In regard to fictional and narrative experimentation, Buckminster Fuller's geodesic dome, Superstudio's "The Continuous Monument," and Rem Koolhaas and Madelon Vriesendorp's "The City of the Captive Globe" are some famous examples.

76   Many early high-rises and bridges were clad and adorned in historicizing styles as advocated by the influential Ecole des Beaux-Arts. It wasn't until the influx of European avant-garde architects into the US during and after the Second World War that structural and technological innovations began to significantly inform the aesthetic language of the building exterior.

77   Barbara Cueto and Bas Hendrikx, eds., *Authenticity? Observations and Artistic Strategies in the Post-Digital Age* (Amsterdam: Making Public Valiz, 2017), 10.

78   Ovid, *Metamorphoses* (London: Penguin Classics, 2004).

Estranged Monument I
The Manhattan Bridge

The Manhattan Bridge, with its eclectic colonnades and triumphant arch, is one such estranged monument. Its majestic gestures were meant to celebrate the marvels of modern engineering and invite visitors to embark upon a river crossing akin to an ancient ceremonial rite. This intention, however, was ill-fated from its beginning, as the necessary axes and boulevards that usually accompany such ritualistic designs and integrate them within the fabric of the city are entirely missing here. Rather than heralding a victorious event or spilling into a spacious plaza from which it could be gazed at admiringly, the arch of the Manhattan Bridge is awkwardly located off-axis from Canal Street, serving merely as an out-of-scale underpass for cars and cutting mercilessly through neighboring Chinatown. The arch and colonnades combine with the rest of the unclad steel bridge to form a rather overdesigned piece of theater, inaccessible and obsolete.

The arch and colonnades of the Manhattan Bridge were hailed by the *New York Times* in 1912 as an apt representation of a "complete, dignified and monumental ensemble, worthy of one of the principal gateways of a great modern city."[79] This ambition to elevate the bridge into a *monument* speaks to the desire to create something eternal and meaningful, a structure that can successfully resist the whims of time and maintain its significance for generations to come. Of course, the irony is that what makes a city modern is precisely its ceaseless redefinition of the meaning and significance of its buildings, often undermining their original intentions and forging unforeseen narratives around them. The monumental qualities of the Manhattan Bridge give way to a whole series of strange spatial, tectonic, and ornamental fragmentations that cry out for new narratives asserting their relevance to the city in its current condition.

The projects dealing with the Manhattan Bridge convey these stories through hybrid artifacts of various scales and functions. These artifacts, in turn, establish a sense of newfound authenticity in and around the bridge, drawing from both the uprooted classical signifiers still present in the arch and colonnades and from the disparate entwinements between the structure and its modern-day environment.

NOTES

79 Christopher Gray, "Gotham's Architecture's Own Dynamic Duo," *New York Times*, December 24, 2006, https://www.nytimes.com/2006/12/24/realestate/24scap.html

Fig. 4.2 Manhattan Bridge Plaza, Canal St. and the Bowery, New York City, circa 1917. (Photograph courtesy Library of Congress.)

The **Manhattan Bridge** was designed by civil engineer Leon Moisseiff and largely completed in 1909 after eight years of construction. Following the Brooklyn and Williamsburg bridges, it became the third suspension structure to span the East River, connecting Manhattan with Brooklyn, which had been recently annexed in 1898. The opulent arched entrance and symmetrical colonnade at the west side of the bridge, completed in 1915, were designed by the prominent architectural firm Carrère and Hastings as a symbolic, welcoming gateway to the city's new borough.

Carrère and Hastings, both of whom had studied at the École des Beaux-Arts, aimed to complement the raw steel trusses and cables of the structure with a more familiar and historically rooted architectural style. References to distinct precedents such as the Porte Saint-Denis in Paris and St. Peter's Square in Rome were intended to synthesize the formal language of technology and innovation with architectural tradition and

significance. Additionally, the sculptor Carl A. Heber was commissioned to embellish the piers of the arch with allegorical sculptures. Reflecting pre-Depression New York's positivist attitude, these adornments represented the Spirit of Industry and the Spirit of Commerce.

Currently, the arch and colonnade are dominated by the highly trafficked intersection of Canal Street and the Bowery—major east-west and north-south axes that impede pedestrian access to the plaza formed by the colonnade. The plaza is surrounded by the dense and diverse urban fabric of Chinatown and the Lower East Side, which particularly effects the architecture beneath the bridge landing. Here, a wealth of misfit and hybrid conditions is generated by the collision of large structural components, small-scale commercial stores and housing, and both ornamental and utilitarian details.

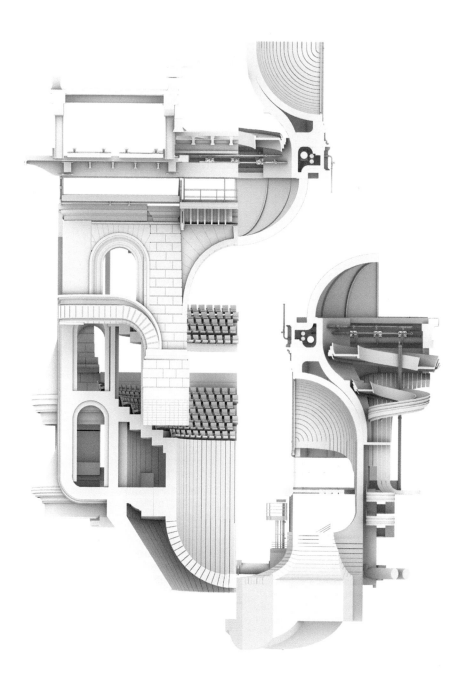

Figs. 4.3, 4.4 Above: John Dai & Jin-Lee Seung. Opposite: Martin Hongbang Chen & Tuo Chen, Manhattan Bridge, renderings, New York Studio, University of Pennsylvania Weitzman School of Design, 2021.

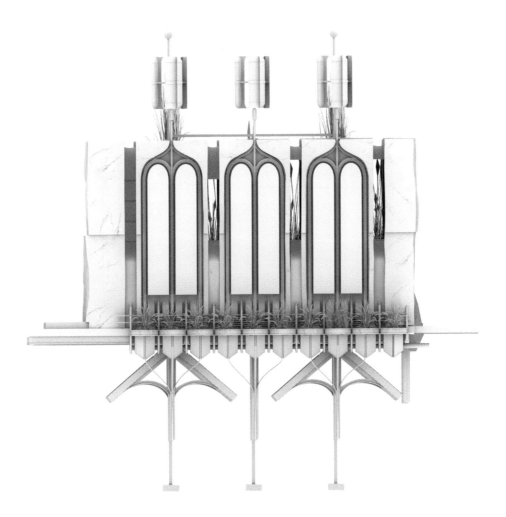

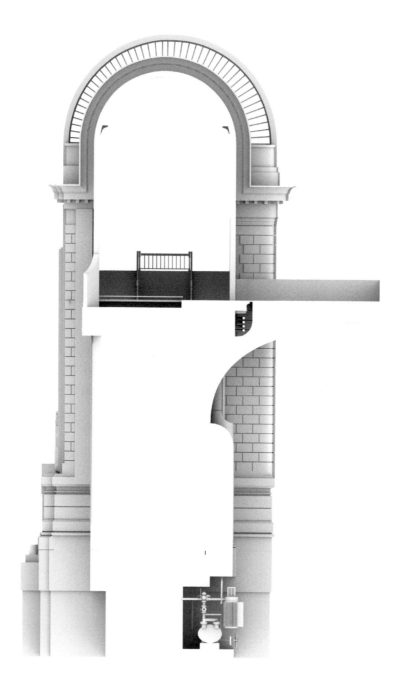

Figs. 4.5, 4.6 Above: Martin Hongbang Chen & Tuo Chen. Opposite: John Dai & Jin-Lee Seung, Manhattan Bridge, renderings, New York Studio, University of Pennsylvania Weitzman School of Design, 2021

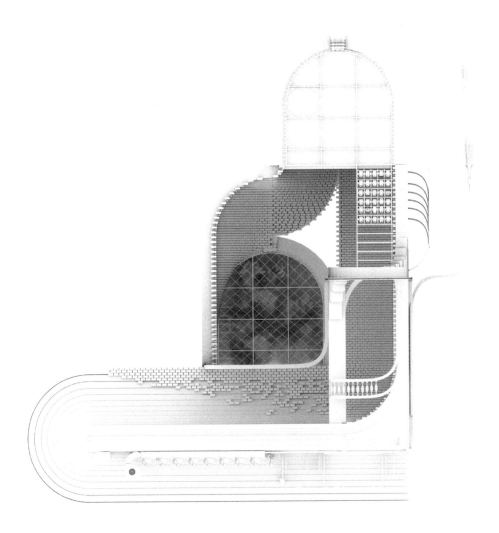

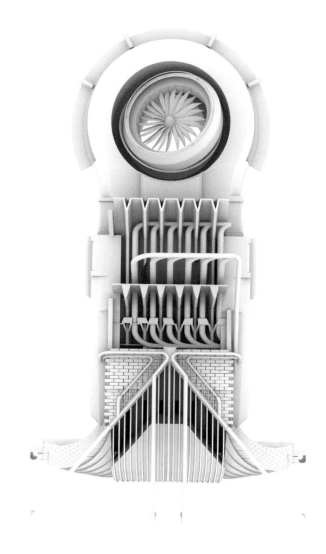

Figs. 4.7, 4.8 Above: Julie McCooey & Diego Ramirez. Opposite: Caryn Yingzhi Chen & Jie Bao, Manhattan Bridge, renderings, New York Studio, University of Pennsylvania Weitzman School of Design, 2021.

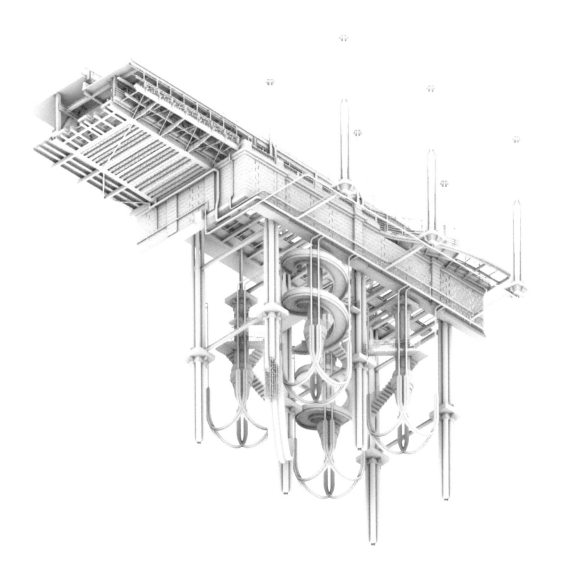

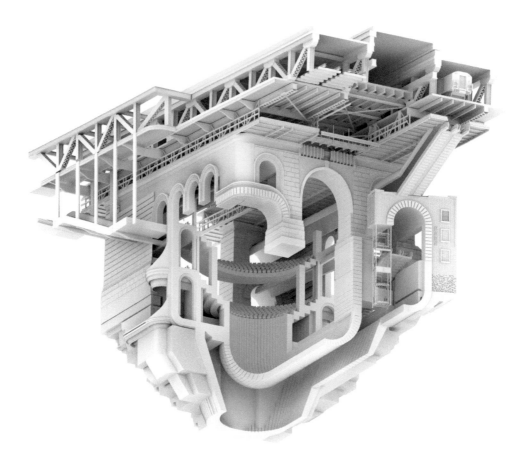

Figs. 4.9, 4.10 Above: John Dai & Jin-Lee Seung. Opposite: Martin Hongbang Chen & Tuo Chen, Manhattan Bridge, renderings, New York Studio, University of Pennsylvania Weitzman School of Design, 2021

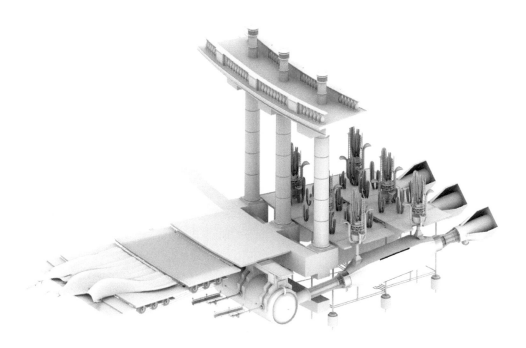

Figs. 4.11, 4.12 Above: Laura Elliott & John Nedeau. Opposite: Bevy Silanqinco & Effy Liu, Manhattan Bridge, renderings, Istanbul Studio, University of Pennsylvania Weitzman School of Design, 2021.

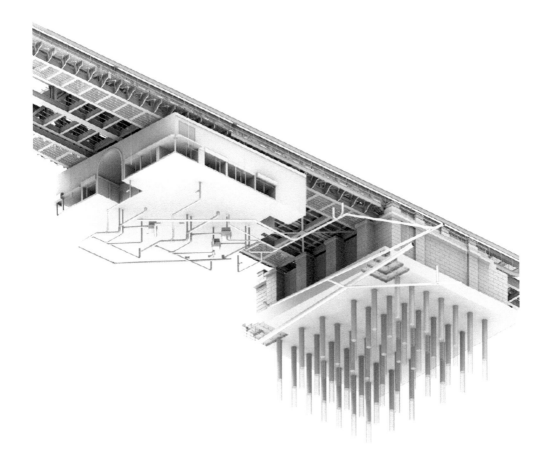

Fig. 4.13 Martin Hongbang Chen & Tuo Chen, Manhattan Bridge, rendering,
New York Studio, University of Pennsylvania Weitzman School of Design, 2021.

The upper driveway of the bridge is converted into a pedestrian promenade, while the arch and colonnade
are separated and transformed into a stand-alone greenhouse.

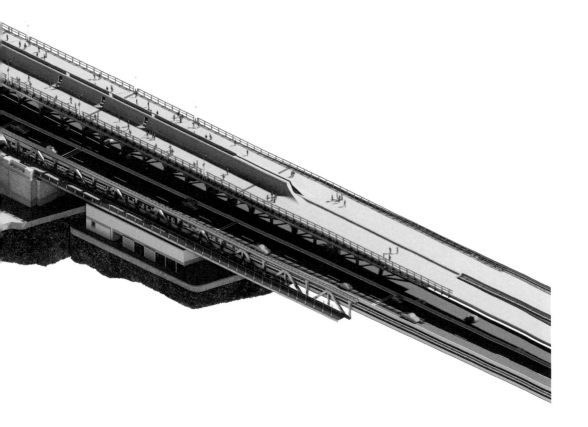

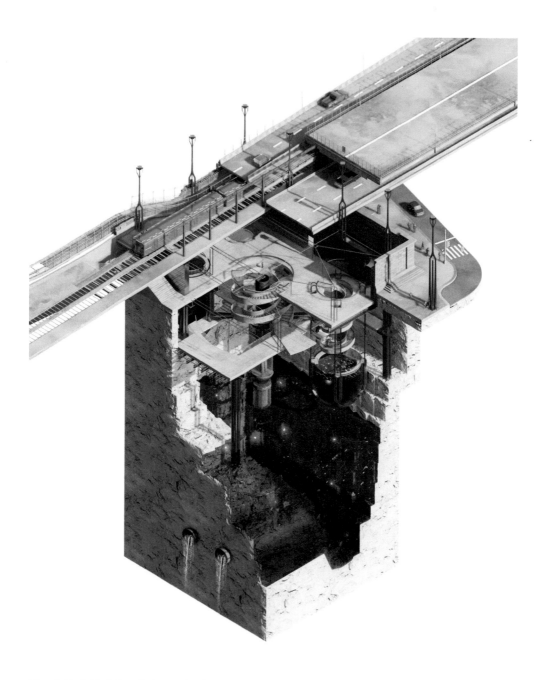

Figs. 4.14, 4.15 Jie Bao & Caryn Yingzhi Chen, Manhattan Bridge, renderings,
New York Studio, University of Pennsylvania Weitzman School of Design, 2021.

The ground below the bridge is partially excavated, flooded with filtered water from the East River,
and transformed into a labyrinthine urban waterpark. Circular stairwells connect the basin with the
street and upper levels of the bridge, making it accessible for pedestrians.

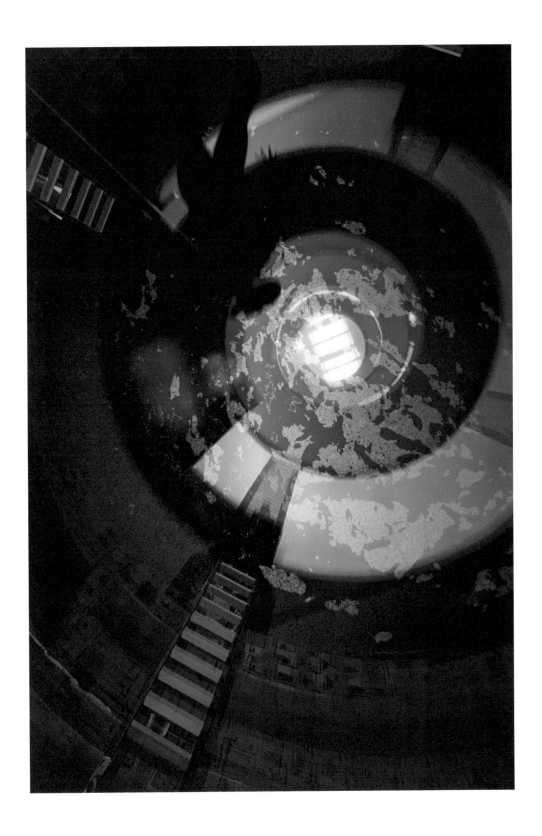

Figs. 4.16, 4.17 John Dai & Jin-Lee Seung, Manhattan Bridge, renderings,
New York Studio, University of Pennsylvania Weitzman School of Design, 2021.

A new performance hall is incorporated into the base of the bridge. The blind windows adorning
the base are transformed into actual windows, allowing views into the illuminated interior.

Estranged Monument II
Early 20th-Century Financial Buildings

The projects in the second "Estranged Monument" section shift their attention from monumental infrastructure to the monumentalization of capital through built form. The decades between the turn of the 20th century and the Great Depression saw an explosion of the banking industry and the establishment and construction of countless new banks and other financial and insurance institutions in New York. Many of these smaller banks and institutions have long since gone out of business–in part, due to the massive consolidation of the banking and finance sectors that took place as the century progressed–and have been left unmaintained, condemned to a slow process of decay. Others have since been converted to serve rather ordinary programmatic needs and purposes, such as pharmacies, lackluster event spaces, or small shopping malls. Yet others have escaped such overt degradation and kept their exteriors intact, with some still serving finance-related purposes. The image of power, control, security, and wealth that they once conveyed through their meticulously composed Beaux-Arts facades, temple-front entrances, columns, pediments, pilasters, and other classicist features, has faded into the city's background and become absorbed within its cornucopia of forms and images.

The question of authenticity is an intriguing and complicated one when it comes to revivalist architecture. Since the aesthetic and symbolic features employed by this architecture hail from different times and places than those of the buildings in question, they function less as markers of authenticity and more like tactical devices for representing the ideologies of their owners and patrons–in this case, the aforementioned capitalist tenets of power, control, security, and wealth. The monumental language of the financial institutions addressed in this final section thus amounts to a double estrangement. First, as historically, locally, and temporally decontextualized building types; and second, as failed iconographic entities that have lost their ability to effectively convey said ideology to their beholders.

The following projects seize on this double estrangement and the ambiguity it imparts on the monumental forms of these former financial buildings. Understanding them as alien artifacts populating the contemporary city or, conversely, as architectural fossils with no clearly identifiable purpose, the projects disregard the buildings' original and current programs and speculate on new ways of utilizing them. The existing ornaments and details, marked by a high level of craft and material value, are examined without bias and, at times, extracted and reassimilated. As is the case with all hybrids in the book, the emerging designs are conceived as fictions, new plots woven into the daily routines of city dwellers that inspire them to engage with the built urban environment in unexpected and novel ways. In New York, these fictions follow a long tradition of experiments to define the future city. However, when it comes to hybrid artifacts, the future is no longer conceived as an idealized projection but rather as the collaborative convergence of the manifold material tensions that are always already present.

Fig. 4.18 Former First National City Bank, New York City, 2021.
(Photograph courtesy Ferda Kolatan.)

Fig. 4.19, 4.20 Above: Former New York County National Bank. Below: Former New York Savings Bank (now CVS pharmacy), New York City, 2021. (Photographs courtesy Ferda Kolatan.)

Fig. 4.21 Interior view of the former New York Savings Bank, New York City, 2021.
(Photograph courtesy Ferda Kolatan.)

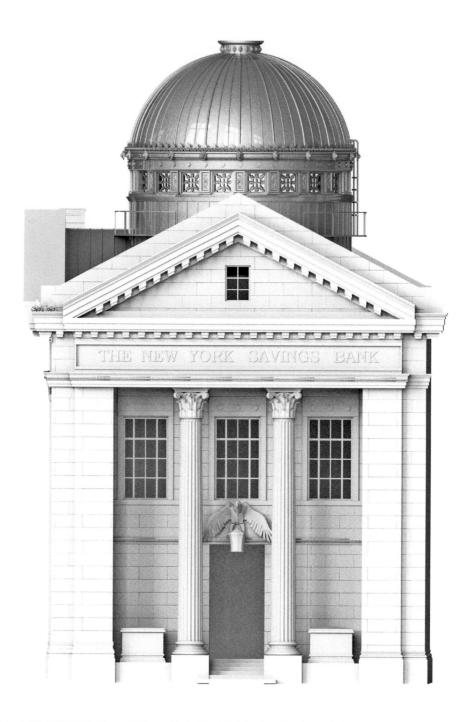

Figs. 4.22, 4.23 Eddie Sheng & Megan York, New York Savings Bank, renderings,
New York Studio, University of Pennsylvania Weitzman School of Design, 2021.

The New York Savings Bank, built between 1896 and '98, currently houses a CVS pharmacy. In this rendering, the opulent dome is extended downward as the center piece of a new DNA sequencing facility. The project subverts the tradition of concealing technological research within anonymous architecture. The precious quality of the inverted dome visualizes the market interest driving this type of research.

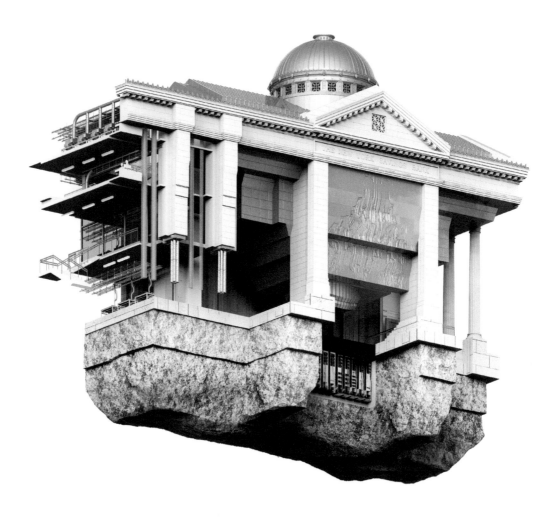

Figs. 4.24, 4.25 Eddie Sheng & Megan York, New York Savings Bank, renderings, New York Studio, University of Pennsylvania Weitzman School of Design, 2021.

The technological infrastructure required for the DNA sequencing is integrated into the modified bank's existing structure and ornamental features.

Figs. 4.26, 4.27 Amber Farrow & Molly Zmich, First National City Bank, renderings, New York Studio, University of Pennsylvania Weitzman School of Design, 2021.

The First National City Bank, originally built in 1927 in a classical/Art Deco style, currently serves as a retail space. The project highlights the former bank's vertical connection with the subway. The bank's Art Deco ornaments mix with the subway's more generic elements (Figs 4.27, 4.28).

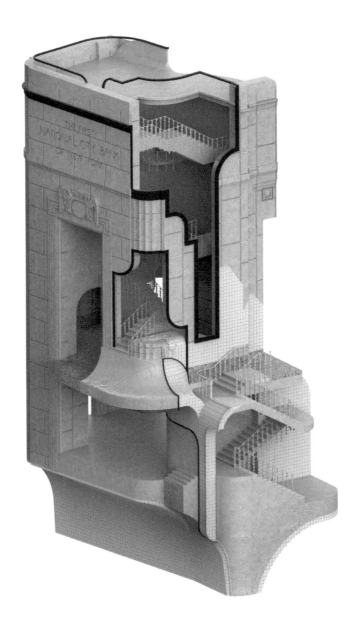

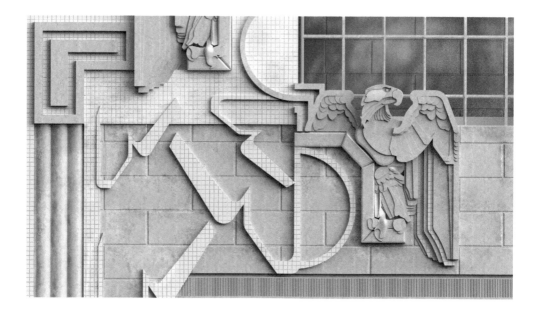

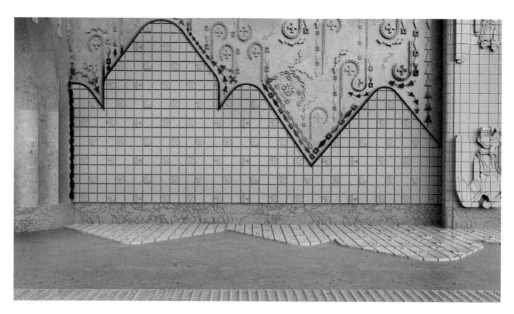

Figs. 4.28, 4.29 Above and opposite: Amber Farrow & Molly Zmich, First National City Bank, renderings, New York Studio, University of Pennsylvania Weitzman School of Design, 2021.

The area surrounding the former bank has become a black market for counterfeit fashion items, including clothing, handbags, shoes, watches, and jewelry. Often, however, these "fakes" are not replicas but hybrids comprising the blended pieces of different items (Fig. 4.29). This practice is reflected in the modified design of the bank.

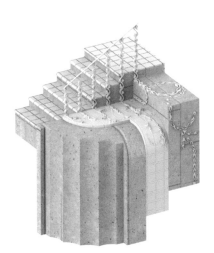

Figs. 4.30, 4.31 Jinghan He, New York County National Bank, renderings,
New York Studio, University of Pennsylvania Weitzman School of Design, 2021.

The New York County National Bank, constructed in 1907, currently houses the Museum of Illusions. This proposal embraces the theme of illusion by integrating a series of dioramas into the bank. The hybrid facade, combining oddly proportioned classical ornaments with a cast-iron structure, showcases various mushrooms and fungi used in medicinal research (Fig. 4.31). The project leverages the bank's facades to frame nature as a scientific and commercial object, to be experienced in the act of window-shopping.

Fig. 4.32 Alexander Brown & Kerry Hohenstein, East River Savings Bank, rendering,
New York Studio, University of Pennsylvania Weitzman School of Design, 2021.

The facade of the former East River Savings Bank, constructed in 1927 and currently home to a CVS pharmacy, is remodeled by duplicating and distorting its classical elements. These transformations are a creative homage to the building's rich history, which has been marked by numerous alterations made to accommodate its expanding size.

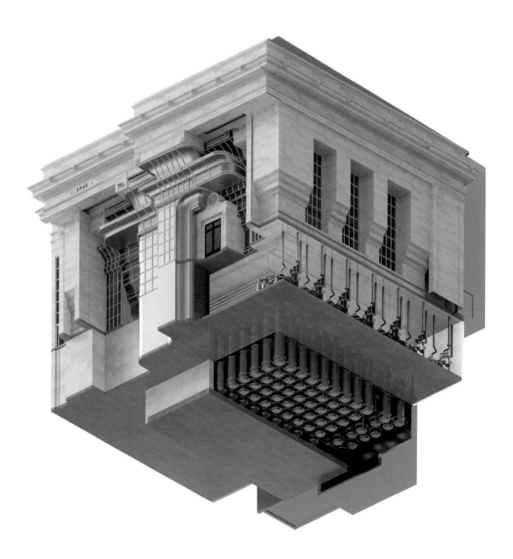

Fig. 4.33 Alexander Brown & Kerry Hohenstein, East River Savings Bank, rendering, New York Studio, University of Pennsylvania Weitzman School of Design, 2021.

The former bank has been repurposed into a cryobiology and cryonics research center. The preservation of organs, organisms, and potentially entire human beings represents a growing field with increasing investments and market interest. Essential mechanical and technological components are integrated into the building's facade and interior to form a unique hybrid structure.

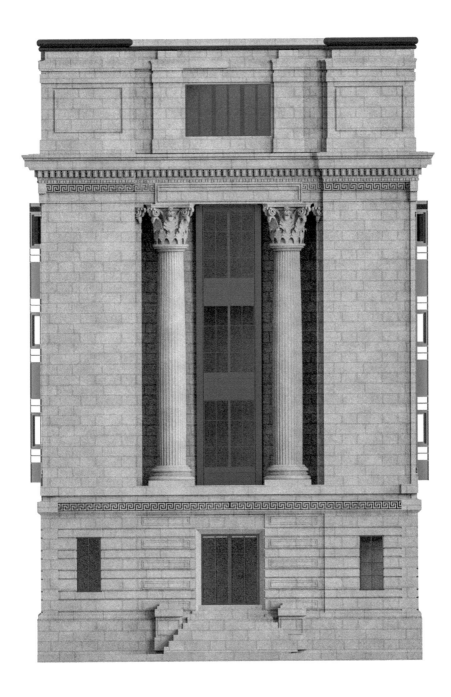

Fig. 4.34 Baoqi Ji & Yuanguang Wang, American Bank Note Company, rendering, New York Studio, University of Pennsylvania Weitzman School of Design, 2020.

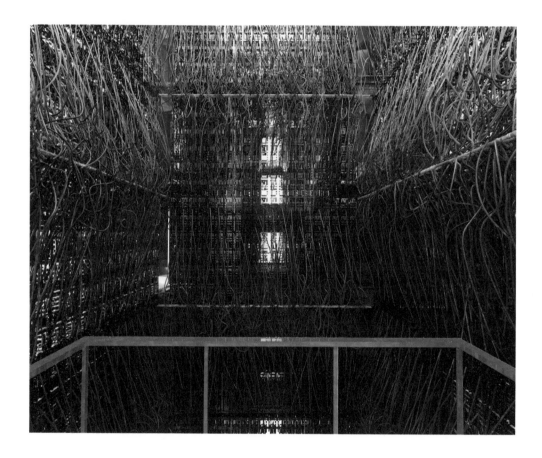

Figs. 4.35, 4.36 Baoqi Ji & Yuanguang Wang, American Bank Note Company, renderings, New York Studio, University of Pennsylvania Weitzman School of Design, 2020.

The former American Bank Note Company building, built in 1908 and currently utilized for offices and private residences, is reimagined as a cryptocurrency mining facility. While the neoclassical exterior (Fig. 4.34) remains unchanged, the inside is retrofitted with the necessary technology. The substantial energy demands of these operations are visually conveyed to the public through an accessible interior resembling a giant server.

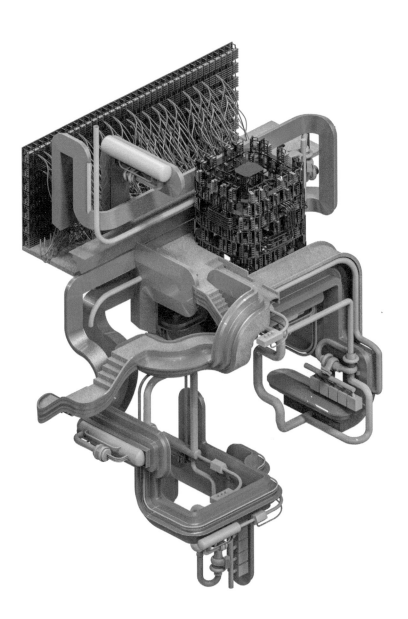

Figs. 4.37, 4.38 Xinyi Chen & Jingyi Zhou, Chamber of Commerce Building, renderings,
New York Studio, University of Pennsylvania Weitzman School of Design, 2020.

The Chamber of Commerce building, completed in 1902 and subsequently repurposed for various
programs, is the foundation for this project. The original boardroom, with its portrait gallery, has inspired
the transformation of the building into a free port for art. Digital art is stored in red-lit servers, while physical
paintings and sculptures are housed and auctioned in the lower half of the building.

Figs. 4.39, 4.40 Glenn Godfrey & Calli Katzelnick, American Stock Exchange Building, renderings, New York Studio, University of Pennsylvania Weitzman School of Design, 2020.

The American Stock Exchange building was erected in 1921. Since 2008, the building has changed ownership multiple times and has been considered for various purposes, including as a hotel and a large event space. Currently, it lacks a specific program. This project transforms the main floors into a giant terrarium by appropriating the building's pneumatic tubes for air and water supply (Fig. 4.40).

Figs. 4.41, 4.42 Glenn Godfrey & Calli Katzelnick, American Stock Exchange Building, renderings, New York Studio, University of Pennsylvania Weitzman School of Design, 2020.

The terrarium protrudes from the existing facade, providing passersby with eerie views of the inside, where various ecosystems, plant species, and microorganisms are cultivated.

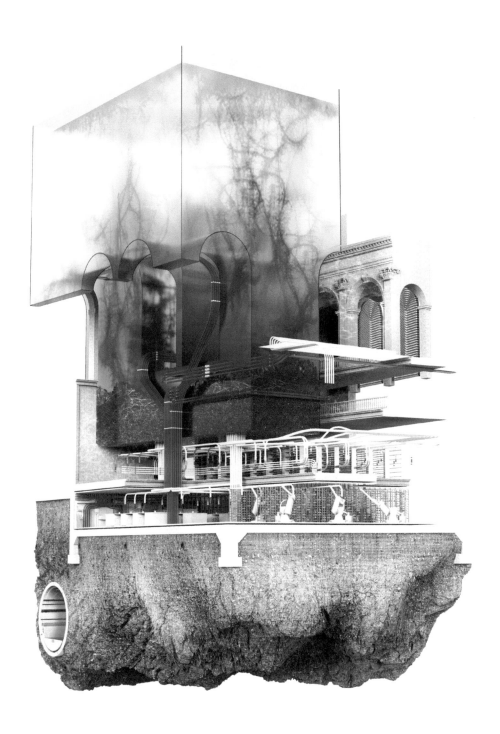

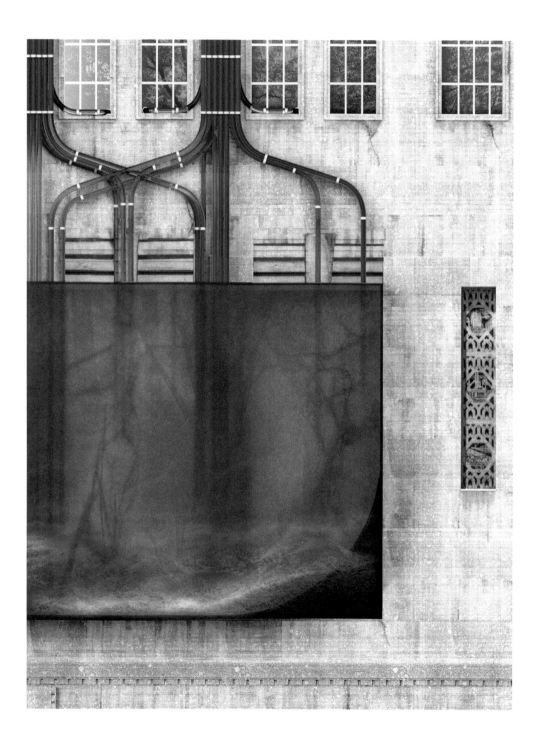

Figs. 4.43, 4.44 Glenn Godfrey & Calli Katzelnick, American Stock Exchange Building, renderings, New York Studio, University of Pennsylvania Weitzman School of Design, 2020

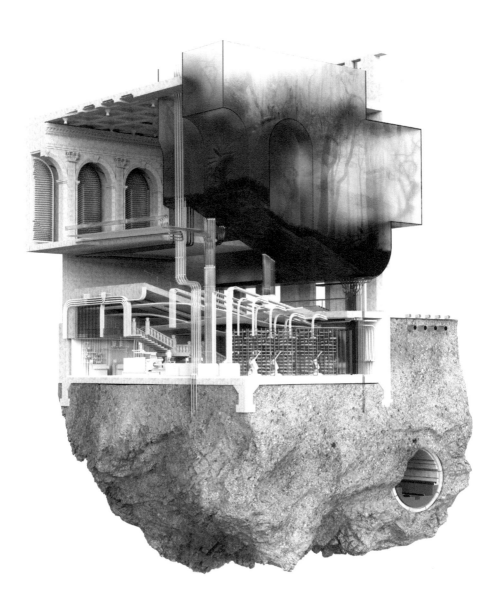

Fig. 4.45 Matt Kohman & Paul
McCoy, Trinity Building, renderings,
New York Studio, University of
Pennsylvania Weitzman School of
Design, 2020.

The Trinity & US Realty building,
one of Manhattan's earliest Neo-
Gothic high-rises, was completed
in 1907. This project reimagines
the tower as a vertical recycling
depot. The roof and facades have
been retrofitted with components
for collection and sorting, adding
another layer of complexity to
the already-eclectic facade, and
transforming the building into a
massive technological device
(see also Fig. 4.1).

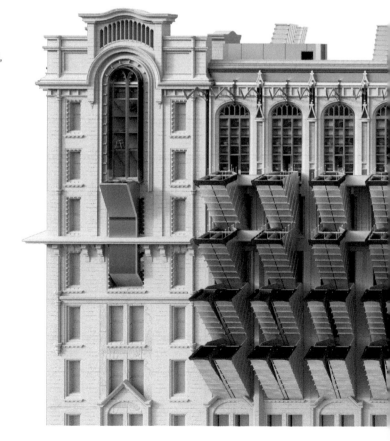

255

Figs. 4.46, 4.47 Matt Kohman & Paul McCoy, Trinity Building, renderings,
New York Studio, University of Pennsylvania Weitzman School of Design, 2020.

The existing mechanical shafts of the tower are repurposed with conveyor systems for the recycling process. Funnel-like structures extend from the roof and facades to receive discarded items dropped by drones. By partially removing the facades, the usually hidden processes of recycling are rendered as a spectacle for passersby on the street and occupants of adjacent buildings.

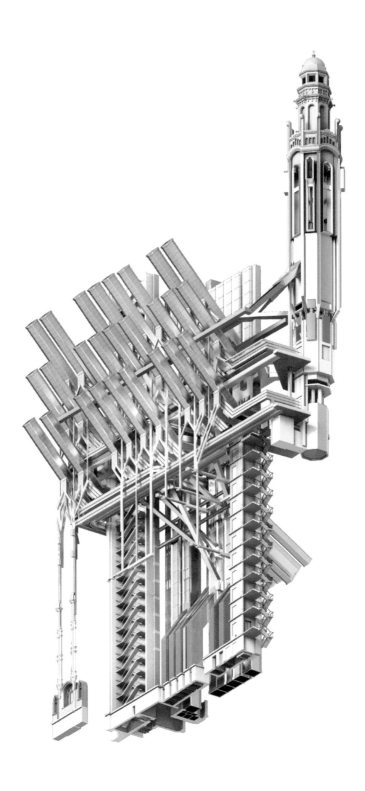

Fig. 4.48 Matt Kohman & Paul McCoy, Trinity Building, detail rendering,
New York Studio, University of Pennsylvania Weitzman School of Design, 2020.

Fig. 4.49 Trinity Building, detail, New York City, 2020. (Photograph courtesy Paul McCoy.)

Acknowledgments

This book would not have been possible without the dedicated efforts of my students at the University of Pennsylvania Weitzman School of Design. Their eagerness to push boundaries and chart unknown territories has been an inspiration. A complete list of their names and studio affiliations is given below. I am deeply indebted to the entire Weitzman community for its creativity, collegiality, and enthusiasm for debate and the free-flowing exchange of ideas. My foremost gratitude goes to Dean Frederick Steiner and former Chair Winka Dubbeldam for their unwavering support, guidance, and friendship over the years.

The ideas and design techniques at the heart of this book have benefitted from countless spirited conversations with colleagues, friends, and mentors. Among my teachers and mentors, my special gratitude goes to Şulan Kolatan, William MacDonald, Laurie Hawkinson, Henry Smith-Miller, Evan Douglis, Vladimir Lalo Nikolic, and the late Detlef Mertins. Among my colleagues and friends, I would particularly like to thank David Ruy, Hernan Diaz Alonso, Karel Klein, Michael Young, Kutan Ayata, Mark Foster Gage, Peter Trummer, Ali Rahim, Florencia Pita, Jason Payne, Michael Osman, Ila Berman, Marcelo Spina, Georgina Huljich, Rhett Russo, Lydia Kallipoliti, Andrew Saunders, Cynthia Davidson, Tom Wiscombe, Elena Manferdini, Marcelyn Gow, Johan Bettum, Ozan Avcı, Silvan Linden, Jörg Leeser, Luc Merx, Andreas Ruby, and Graham Harman.

My partners at SU11 Architecture + Design, Erich Schoenenberger and Hart Marlow, have been critical in fostering the kind of atmosphere within which practice and experimentation converge and thrive. I am grateful for my wonderful editor, Lily Bartle, and graphic designers Esen Karol and Una Aaro for helping me over the hurdles of designing a book. A very special thank you goes to Aslıhan Ünaldı, whose steadfast encouragement and inquisitive mind have helped me greatly in structuring my thoughts.

I owe further gratitude to my skillful teaching assistants Michael Zimmerman, Caleb Ehly, and Megan York. I am deeply indebted to those who collaborated on and sponsored the studios in Cairo and Istanbul. It was the initiative of Aly Abouzeid, who invited us to Egypt in 2016/'17, that prompted the thoughts and research that would eventually culminate in this book. The expertise and guidance of Eng. Ibrahim Mehlib, Dr. Laila Iskandar, Eng. Mohamed Abu Saeda, Dr. Gihane Zaki, Dr. Haby Hosney, and Ahmed Zaazaa were invaluable to these studios. The Istanbul studios were made possible by the generous help of Gökhan Avcioğlu and the GAD Foundation. My gratitude goes to the amazing GAD team and, in particular, to Gökhan Karakuş, Gizem Geylan, Gürkan Güney, Sinem Altay, Ece Başkan, Seda Tuğutlu, Ali Geylan, Deniz Ergan, Mina Barut, and the late Alpaslan Ataman.

Design Studios

Cairo, Spring 2016: Fan Cao, Dunbee Choi, Joseph Giampietro, Heng Gu, Yanghui Huang, Hyemi Kang, Grace Kim, Brett Lee, Rachel Lee, Hadeel Mohammad, Chi Zhang, and Xinyue Zhang. Teaching Assistant: Michael Zimmerman.

Cairo, Spring 2017: Aly Abouzeid, John Darby, Carrie Frattali, Angela Huang, Kyuhun Kim, Meari Kim, Angeliki Mavroleon, Rosanna Pitarresi, Kaikang Shen, Alex Tahinos, Angeliki Tzifa, and Jianbo Zhong. Teaching Assistant: Michael Zimmerman.

Cairo, Fall 2017: Lauren Aguilar, Alexander Bahr, Ryan Barnette, Lillian Candela, Jin Woo Lee, Xuechuan Qin, Jennifer Rokoff, Mana Sazegara, Yiqun Shen, Siqi Wang, Shuxin Wu, and Yi Yan. Teaching Assistant: Michael Zimmerman.

Istanbul, Spring 2018: Carla Bonilla, Zhuoqing Cai, Wenjia Go, Andrew Homick, Chae Young Kim, Yang Li, Haeyun Kwon, Yibo Ma, Neera Sharma, Yiren Weng, Mengqi Xu, Zehua Zhang, and Yuanyi Zhou. Teaching Assistant: Michael Zimmerman.

Istanbul, Spring 2019: Christian Cueva, Andrew Homick, Agata Jakubowska, Xuexia Li, Andrew Matia, Difei Shan, Qianni Shi, Emily Sun, Wenhao Xu, Sanxing Zhao, Yangxunxun Zhou, and Sihan Zhu. Teaching Assistant: Michael Zimmerman.

Istanbul, Fall 2019: Zoe Cennami, Adriana Davis, Caleb Ehly, Michelle Eshelman, Jiancheng Gu, Xiaoqing Gua, Ryan Henriksen, Tae Hyung, Ira Kapaj, Joonsung Lee, Jingwen Luo, Margarida Mota, Kimberly Shoemaker, and Jennifer Minjee Son. Teaching Assistant: Michael Zimmerman.

New York, Fall 2020: Xinyi Chen, Glenn Godfrey, Baoqi Ji, Calli Katzelnick, Matt Kohman, Zhihui Li, Paul McCoy, Yiding Wang, Yuanguang Wang, Yufei Wang, Yang Yang, and Jingyi Zhou. Teaching Assistant: Caleb Ehly.

New York, Spring 2021: Alexander Brown, Bridget Farley, Amber Farrow, Jinghan He, Kerry Hohenstein, Eddie Sheng, Katharine Vavilov, Megan York, and Molly Zmich. Teaching Assistant: Caleb Ehly.

New York, Fall 2021: Jie Bao, Hongbang Chen, Yingzhi Chen, Tuo Chen, John Dai, Laura Elliott, Effy Liu, Julie McCooey, John Nedeau, Diego Ramirez, Jin-Lee Seung, and Bevy Silanqinco. Teaching Assistant: Megan York.

Index

Note: italic page numbers indicate figures; page number followed by n refer to notes.

Abouzeid, Aly *196*, *197*
adaptive reuse 3, 11–12, 18n8
aesthetics 14–17, 22, 142, 146, 150; and defamiliarization 15–16; of informal settlements 146, 150; part-to-whole 27
affinities 44, 45, 45n50; Islamic-Christian/East-West *51*, *56*, *57*
Alberti, Leon Battista 27
ambiguity 71, 207, 226
American Bank Note Company (New York) *243*, *244*, *245*
American Stock Exchange Building (New York) *248*, *249*, *250*, *251*, *252*, *253*
animals in cities 104–107, 158
Anthropocene 42, 126, 132n63
anthropocentrism 5, 6n3, 29n28, 130
archaeology 20–21, 32
arches/domes of Istanbul *47*, *49*, *52*, 86, 87–94, *87*, *88*, *89*, *90*, *91*, *92–93*; hybrid artifacts of *46*, *53*, *62*
architectural fantasy drawings 6, 30–35, *31*; and capriccios 6, 32–33, 34, 35; and collage 34–35; and rocailles 6, 33–34, *34*, 35, 35n44
architectural icons 42
architectural oddities 1–4; and concept of real 3–4; as global phenomenon 3; and liminal space 4; as overlooked features 1–2; potential for design of 2–3; reappraisal of, framework for 2–3; ubiquity of 1
architecture: as background/foreground 45; criteria/ordering principles for 2, 4, 5, 9; spatial dimension of 44, 45n51; and value judgements 142
art 15–16, 19n14, *see also* architectural fantasy drawings; visual arts
artifacts 20–21, 30
artification 16–17
assemblies/assemblages 2, 5, 23n22, 34; and hybrids, distinction between 41; and part-to-whole organization 24
assets 3, 140, 144
authenticity 206–207, 226

Badiou, Alan 3, 4, 6n2
Bao, Jie *215*, *222*, *223*
bazaars 42, 83, 84, 172–173, *see also* Büyük Valide Han

Beaux-Arts style 8, 207n7, 209, 226

Belvedere, The (Choi/Giampietro, Cairo, 2016) 152–153, *153*

Bennett, Jane 14

Bilgi University (Istanbul) *59*

Bonilla, Carla *26, 71, 72*

Bowery, the (New York) 207n72, 209, *209*

bridges of Cairo 140, 141–142, 180–201, *181*; Casr El Nil Bridge 182, *182, 184–185, 186, 187, 188–189, 190, 191*; as hazards for pedestrians 180, 183; Imbaba Bridge 182, *182, 192, 196, 197, 198, 199, 200–201*; and local material practices 13; and Ponte Vecchio (Florence) 183; repurposing of (Yan/Wang, 2017) *143*; 6th of October Bridge 182, *182, 193, 194, 195*

Brown, Alexander *240–241, 242*

building regulations 4

building–demolition–rebuilding cycle 11, 12

Büyük Valide Han (Istanbul) 42, 81–107, *81, 82*; alterations to 86, *97*; Altered Arches project 86, 87–94, *87, 88, 89, 90, 91, 92–93*; Bird Sanctuary project 86–87, 104–109, *105, 106, 107, 108, 109*; courtyards/stairways of 84, *90, 91, 95*, 96, *99*; decline of 82, 84, 85; Nested Pavilion project 86, 94–98, *94, 95, 96*; Performing Han project 86, 98–103, *99, 100, 101, 102, 103*; shops in 82, 83, 84, 85, 86, 94, 98, 104; site of 84–87, *85*; workshops in 98

Cai, Zhuoqing *51*

Cairo (Egypt) 6, 137–201; bridges in *see* bridges of Cairo; informal settlements in *see* informal settlements (Cairo); and Istanbul, compared 139–140; local techniques/protocols in 18n4; Nile Corniche 180, 183; poverty in 139, 140, 144, 149, 152, 154, 166; and Real Fictions concept 140, 142; renovation of 180, 183n71; traffic congestion in 139, 141, 166, 180; trash collection/recycling in 149–150, *151*, 164; urban growth in 139, 140, 148, 150n66, 174; Zamalek Island 141, 182

calling-power 14, 17, 18n10

Cao, Fan *163, 176, 178, 179*

capitalism 6n2, 9, 18n5, 226

capriccio 6, 32–33, 34, 35

carbon footprint/emissions 6, 10–11, 12, 158; and embodied/operational carbon 11, 18n7

Carceri etchings (Piranesi) 32, 35nn37,38

Carrère and Hastings 209

Casr El Nil Bridge (Cairo) 182, *182, 184–185, 186, 187, 188–189, 190, 191*

Cave Monastery of Saint Simon (Manshiyat Naser, Cairo) 149, *150*

Cennami, Zoe *61, 105, 106, 107, 108*

Chamber of Commerce Building (New York) *246, 247*

Chen, Martin Hongbang *212, 213, 217, 220–221*

Chen, Tuo *212, 217, 220–221*

Chen, Xinyi *246, 247*

Choi, Dunbee *153, 155*

cities: animals in 104–107, 158; complexity/disorderliness of 3, 8; concept of 2; flattening of 10

classical modernism 2, 146, 152

classicism 5, 6n3

collaborative acts 14, 18n6, 26, 29, 144, 145

collage 34–35

Conjoined Mansion, The (Kang/Lee, 2016) 160–161, *161*

Conveyor House, The (Gu/Zhang, 2016) 164–165, *165*

corner details, hybrid artifact of (Istanbul) *55*

courtyard, sectional model of (Istanbul, Ehly/Lee, 2019) *7*

Cueto, Barbara 206–207

culture 2, 3, 6, 12–14; and pluralism 22, 29

customs 2, 12, 13, 39, 70, 83

Dai, John *210, 211, 213, 216, 224, 225*

Darby, John *196, 197*

decontextualization 17, 26, 29

Decorated Wall (Ezbet Khayrallah, Cairo) *167*, 168–172, *169, 170, 171*

decorative elements 20, 33, *65*

defamiliarization 15, 16, 17, *see also* estrangement

democratization of objects 41, 43n48

digital world 22, 29, 29n34

Dolmabahçe Palace (Istanbul) *57*

East River Savings Bank (New York) *240–241, 242*

ebru painting 72, 121, *128*

Ehly, Caleb *7, 48, 55, 58, 63, 94, 95, 96*

electrical boxes 10

Elliott, Laura *218*

embodied carbon 11, 18n7

Eminönü district (Istanbul) *47*, 84, *see also* Büyük Valide Han

empathy 14, 130

Empson, William 71

Enlightenment 22, 126–128

environmental degradation 10, 11, 119, 128–130, 139

estrangement 15, 17

Ezbet Khayrallah (Cairo) 14, *15*, 142, 166–174; and Decorated Wall *167*, 168–172, *169, 170, 171, see also* Ring Road

facades 8, 10, 13; as objects 24–26, *26*

Farrow, Amber *31, 234, 235, 236, 237*

fiction 30, *see also* architectural fantasy drawing

financial buildings of New York 206, 226–259, *227, 228, 229*; American Bank Note
   Company *243, 244, 245*; American Stock Exchange *248, 249, 250, 251, 252, 253*;
   Chamber of Commerce *246, 247*; East River Savings Bank *240–241, 242*; First
   National City Bank *227, 234, 235, 236, 237*; New York County National Bank *16,228,
   238, 239*; New York Savings Bank *228, 229, 230, 231, 232, 233*; Trinity Building *254–
   255, 256, 257, 258, 259*

First National City Bank (New York) *227, 234, 235, 236, 237*

floral tiling, hybrid artifact of (Istanbul) *48*

follies, architectural 62, *119*, 132n, *133*, 182

fountains 13, *34, 57, 64*, 70, *79*, 79n57

Frattali, Carrie *188–189, 190, 191*

functionalism 5, 9, 152

Gabkhana (Cairo) 141, 174–179; inaccessibility of 174; restoration plans for 174,
   177n69; site of 174–175, *174, 175*; Vault 176–177, *177*

gardens 123–124, 132n59, *see also* Machinic Garden

gentrification 141, 144

Giampietro, Joseph *153, 155*

Go, Wenjia *56, 65, 75, 76, 77, 78*

Godfrey, Glenn *248, 249, 250, 251, 252, 253*

Golden Horn coast (Istanbul) 70, 110, 112

graffiti 12, 15–16, 17, 18n9

Greece, ancient 21, 27, 29n30, 39

greenhouse gases *see* carbon footprint/emissions

Gu, Eric Jiancheng *99, 100, 101, 102, 103*

Gu, Heng *159*

Gua, Xiaoqing *99, 100, 101, 102, 103*

Hagia Sophia (Istanbul) 78n53, 110

hans (Istanbul) 20, *21*, 83, *see also* Büyük Valide Han

Harman, Graham 18n6, 27, 29n28

He, Jinghan *238, 239*

Heinich, Nathalie 17

Hendrikx, Bas 206–207

Henriksen, Ryan *21, 87, 88, 89, 90, 91, 92–93*

hierarchical classifications 5, 9, 16, 22–23; and object-to-object relationships 27, 29

hoarding 14–15

Hohenstein, Kerry *240–241, 242*

Homick, Andrew *5, 46, 133, 134–135*

Huang, Angela *184–185, 186, 187*

Huang, Yanghui *173*

Hybrid Artifact (Kim/Lee, 2016) *vi*
hybrid artifacts *vi*, 4, *7*, 12, 20–23, *25*, 182, 227; and authenticity 206; design of *see*
  hybrid design; as fantasy *see* architectural fantasy drawings; and object-to-object
  relationships 29; and parts-to-whole relationships 5, 24; and photographs 44–45
hybrid design 10, 20, 30; and ambiguity 71; guidelines for models 40–42
hybrids 3, 4; and assemblages, distinction between 41; and capacity to shock 22, 23n22;
  defined/use of term 21, 23n21; and modernity 22–23; neglected in architecture 22, *see
  also* nature–culture hybridity; technological hybrids
Hyung, Tae *21, 87, 88, 89, 90, 91, 92–93*

icons, architectural 42
Imbaba Bridge (Cairo) 182, *182, 192, 196, 197, 198, 199, 200–201*
Imperial Haliç Shipyard (Istanbul) 42, *60*, 110–135; coloured/textural effects in
  120–122; facade of *111*; history of 111; and Machinic Garden *see* Machinic Garden;
  mechanical devices in 114–115, *114, 115*; shops in 110; site of 110, 112–115, *113*;
  water-based processes in 116–119, *116, 117, 118, 119*
industrial equipment *58*, 132n58, *see also* Machinic Garden
industrial site conversion 42, 110–112
industrialization 21, 102, 121
Informal Assets Catalogue 140–141, *145*, 146–149, *147*, 152–165; aim of 148–149;
  Belvedere, The (Choi/Giampietro, 2016) 152–153, *153*; Conjoined Mansion, The
  (Kang/Lee, 2016) 160–161, *161*; Conveyor House, The (Gu/Zhang, 2016) 164–165,
  165; and Highway Underbelly rendering (Huang/Zhang, 2016) *173*; Loft, The
  (Cao/Mohammad, 2016) 162–163, *163*; and real estate advertising 146–147; Rock,
  The (Kim/Lee, 2016) 156–157, *157*; Urban Barn (Gu/Zhang, 2016) 158–159, *159*;
  Veiled Villa, The (Choi/Giampietro, 2016) 154–155, *155*
informal settlements (Cairo) *138*, 140, 144–179; aesthetics/style of 145, 146, 150; as
  assets 140, 144, 147, 148; entrepreneurialism in 149, 169; and Gabkhana 141; and
  gentrification 141, 144; and Informal Assets Catalogue *see* Informal Assets
  Catalogue; municipal neglect of 166; stigmatization of 141, 144, 152, *see also* Ezbet
  Khairallah; Manshiyat Naser
infrastructure 6, 8, 11, 18n4, 20, 26, 172
Istabl Antar (Cairo) *see* Gabkhana
Istanbul (Turkey) 6, *9*, 38–135; arches/domes in *see* arches/domes of Istanbul; Bilgi
  University *59*; and Cairo, compared 139–140; corner details in, hybrid artifact of *55*;
  courtyard in, sectional model of (Ehly/Lee, 2019) *7*; Dolmabahçe Palace *57*;
  East-West hybrids in *51, 56, 57*; Eminönü district *47*; floral tiling in, hybrid artifact
  of *48*; fountains in *57, 64*, 70, *79*, 79nn54,57; Galata district 111, 112, *113*, 114; Golden
  Horn coast 70, 110, 112; Grand Bazaar 83, 84; guidelines for models 40–42; Hagia
  Sophia 78n53, 110; Haliç Shipyard *see* Imperial Haliç Shipyard; hans in *see* hans;
  history of 39, 43n46; industrial equipment/concrete in, hybrid artifact of *58*; Kethüda
  Yusuf Efendi Çesmesi *13*; Kılıç Ali Paşa Mosque 73, 79nn54,55; Küçük Ayasofya

Mosque *50*; landmarking in 40, 42, 70, 71–72, 82–84; light fixture in, hybrid artifact of *51*; lintel reliefs in, hybrid artifact of *63*; local techniques/protocols in 18n4; marble in *63*; muqarnas in *49, 51, 56, 62, 64*, 79n56; Nuruosmaniye Mosque *51*; Nusretiye Mosque *38*; Ottoman armory facade in *26*; park in, hybrid artifact of *65*; Rainbow Stairs 18n9; residential building in, sectional model of *5*; and ribbing in mosque *50*; security booth in 10, *11*; sprinkler head/Ottoman pavilion in, hybrid artifact of *56*; Süleymaniye Mosque *49, 62*, 110; Tophane *see* Tophane district; Topkapı Palace *54, 56*; weathering in, hybrid artifact of *61*

Jakubowska, Agata *122*
Ji, Baoqi *243, 244, 245*

Kang, Hyemi *161*
Kapaj, Ira *81*
Katzelnick, Calli *248, 249, 250, 251, 252, 253*
Kethüda Yusuf Efendi Çesmesi (Istanbul) *13*
Kılıç Ali Paşa Mosque (Istanbul) 73, 79nn54,55
Kim, Chae Young *79*
Kim, Grace *vi, 157, 169, 170, 171*
Kim, Kyuhun *192, 194, 195*
Kim, Meari *192, 194, 195*
Kimball, Fiske 33
Kohman, Matt *204, 254–255, 256, 257, 258*
Koolhaas, Rem 35n45, 207n75
Küçük Ayasofya Mosque (Istanbul) *50*
Kwon, Haeyun *79*

landmarking 40, 42, 70, 71–72, 82–84
Lang, Fritz 205, 207n74
Latour, Bruno 23, 132n63
Le Corbusier 29n32
Lee, Brett *161, 176, 178, 179*
Lee, Joonsung *7, 48, 55, 58, 63, 94, 95, 96*
Lee, Rachel *vi, 157, 169, 170, 171*
leisure space 99, 104, 110, 112, 146, 180, 183
Li, Xuexia *125, 126, 127, 130*
Li, Yang *72*
Libera, Adalberto 156
light fixture, hybrid artifact of (Istanbul) *51*
liminal space 4, 124, 168
lintel reliefs, hybrid artifact of (Istanbul) *63*
Liu, Effy *219*

local material practices 2, *15*, 18n4, 183
Loft, The (Cao/Mohammad, 2016) 162–163, *163*
Luo, Jingwen *53*, *62*

Ma, Yibo *73*
McCooey, Julie *214*
McCoy, Paul *204*, *254–255*, *256*, *257*, *258*
Machinic Garden (Imperial Haliç Shipyard, Istanbul) 112, 123–135; and ebru painting 121, 122, *128*; follies in *119*, *133*; as nature–technology amalgamation 126; and painterly effects *120*, *121*, *122*, *125*, *126*, *127*; and water-based processes *116*, *117*, *118*, *119*, *123*, *130*, *131*
Manhattan (New York) 205, 206, 207n72; Bowery, the 207n72, 209, *209*
Manhattan Bridge (New York) 206, 208–225; history/style of 209; renderings of *210–225*
Manshiyat Naser (Cairo) 140, 141, 142, *148*, 149–165; Belvedere, The (Choi/Giampietro, 2016) 152–153, *153*; and Cave Monastery of Saint Simon 149, 150, *150*; Conjoined Mansion, The (Kang/Lee, 2016) 160–161, *161*; Conveyor House, The (Gu/Zhang, 2016) 164–165, *165*; entrepreneurialism in 149; Loft, The (Cao/Mohammad, 2016) 162–163, *163*; Rock, The (Kim/Lee, 2016) 156–157, *157*; Urban Barn (Gu/Zhang, 2016) 158–159, *159*; Veiled Villa, The (Choi/Giampietro, 2016) 154–155, *155*; and Zabbaleen garbage collectors 149–150, 150n67, *151*
marginalized communities 141, 142, *see also* informal settlements
Matia, Andrew *116*
Mavroleon, Angeliki *193*, *198*, *199*, *200–201*
meaning in architecture 71–72
Meissonnier, Juste-Aurèle 34
Metamorphoses (Ovid) 1, 207
Metropolis (Lang, 1927) 205, 207n74
misfits 3–4, 6, 8–17; and aesthetics 14–17; and collaborative acts 26; and culture 12–14; and environment 10–12; as subversive 8; as symptoms of dysfunction/failure 9; ubiquity of 1, 8
models: guidelines for 40–42
modernity 23, 130, 139
Mohammad, Hadeel *163*
Mokattam Village (Cairo) 149–150, 150n67, *151*, 164
Mondon, Jean 34, *34*
Mota, Margarida *61*, *105*, *106*, *107*, *108*
muqarnas *49*, *51*, *56*, *62*, *64*, 79n56

nature–culture hybridity 27, 42, *65*; and gardens 123, 124–126
nature–technology hybridity 21–22, 23nn21,22, *116*, 124–126, 132nn61,63
Nedeau, John *218*
New York County National Bank *16*, *228*, *238*, *239*

New York Savings Bank *228, 229, 230, 231, 232, 233*

New York (US) 6, 203–259; and authenticity 206–207, 226; banks in *see* financial buildings of New York; experimentation/reinvention in 205–206, 207n75; history of 205, 207n72; local techniques/protocols in 18n4; Trinity Building *204*

Nile Corniche (Cairo) 180, 183

non-architecture 2, 4, 11–12, 17, 44

Nuruosmaniye Mosque (Istanbul) *51*

Nusretiye Mosque, Istanbul (Balyan, 1822–26) *38*

object-to-object relationships 28–29, 30, 33–34; as non-hierarchical 27, 29, 34

objects 24–29; and change 17; democratization of 41, 43n48; and history 10; and hoarding 14–15; as urban categorizing principle 5, 9–10, 18n6

offices 110, *111*, 162, *195, 244*

Ottoman armory facade (Istanbul, Bonilla/Yang, 2018) *26*

Ovid 1, 207

Panini, Giovanni Paolo 32

parts-to-whole relationships 5, 24, 27, 28, 33

photomontages 42, *72, 73, 74, 78, 92, 119, 123, 133*

Piazza Navona (Panini) 32

Piranesi 32, 35n37

Pitarresi, Rosanna *193, 198, 199, 200–201*

planning policies 2, 14

pollution 10, 116, 118, 126

Ponte Vecchio (Florence) 183

postindustrial city 2, 6, 102, 110–112, 123

postmodernism 22, 28, 29

poverty 139, 140, 144, 149, 152, 154, 166

public parks *65*, 74–75, *74, 75, 78*, 112, 123, 132n58, 207n75

purity, architectural 5, 6n3

Rainbow Stairs (Istanbul) 18n9

Ramirez, Diego *214*

real estate advertising 146, 147, 150n65

real, the 3–4, 6n2

reappropriation 3, 10, 11, 12, 26, *125*

recycled waste 149–150, 150n67, *151*, 164

Renaissance 27, 30, 32

Rendez-vous, Le (Aveline, after Mondon, 1736) *34*

renewable energy 10–11

retail spaces *see* shops

reuse, adaptive 3, 11–12, 18n8

Ring Road (Ezbet Khayrallah, Cairo) 141, 166–168, *166, 167, 174*; and Decorate Wall *see* Decorated Wall; negative impact of 166–167, 172, 173–174; Underbelly of 172–174, *173*
rocaille 6, 33–34, *34*, 35, 35n44
Rock, The (Kim/Lee, 2016) 156–157, *157*
Rococo style 33, 35nn42,44

Saint Simon, Cave Monastery of (Cairo) 149, 150, *150*
Sanatkarlar Park (Istanbul) 74–78, *74, 75, 76, 77, 78*
science 21–22, 23, 126–128, 130, 132n64
security cameras 10, *56*
Seung, Jin-Lee *210, 211, 213, 216, 224, 225*
Shapiro, Robert 17
Sharma, Neera *71, 72*
Sheng, Eddie *230, 231, 232, 233*
Shklovsky, Viktor 15–16
Shoemaker, Kimberley *81*
shops 79n54, 110, *234, see also* bazaars
sidewalks 9, 26
Silanqinco, Bevy *219*
6th of October Bridge (Cairo) 182, *182, 193, 194, 195*
social change 35; and artification 17
Son, Jennifer Minjee *53, 62*
Stair Artifact (Farrow/Zmich, 2021) *31*
stairways 18n9, 84, *90, 91*
Steil, Lucien 32–33
storylines/storytelling 8, 18n4, 21, 124
street art 12, 18n9
streetlights 26, 74
Süleymaniye Mosque (Istanbul) *49, 62*, 110
Sun, Emily *57, 120*
Superstudio 35n45, 207n75
sustainability 8, 10–11

Tadgell, Christopher 33
Tahinos, Alex *184–185, 186, 187*
technological hybrids 21–22, 23nn21,22, *116*, 124–126, 132nn61,63
three-dimensional models 41, 43n49
tiling *48*
Tophane district (Istanbul) 70–80, 79n54; bleachers 73–74, *73*; foundry *72, 73, 74*, 79n54; Kılıç Ali Paşa Mosque 73, 79nn54,55; Sanatkarlar Park 74–78, *74, 75, 76, 77, 78*; Tophane Fountain *64*, 79n54; tram station 26, *71, 72, 73*

Topkapı Palace (Istanbul) *54*, *56*
traffic congestion 6, 139, 141, 166, 180
Tzifa, Angeliki *188–189*, *190*, *191*

Urban Barn (Gu/Zhang, 2016) 158–159, *159*
urban growth 9, 111, 139, 140, 150n66, 174
urban renewal 3, 18n5, 42, 206, 207n75

Veiled Villa, The (Choi/Giampietro, 2016) 154–155, *155*
Venturi, Robert 20
visual arts *15*, 21, 44
Vitruvius 27

Wang, Siqi *143*
Wang, Yuanguang *243*, *244*, *245*
waste management 149–150, 150n67, *151*, 164
waste production 6, 10
weathering *61*, 98, *118*, *124*, 177
Weng, Yiren *5*
Western tradition 6n3, 22, 23n23
Wilton-Ehly, John 30, 32
windows 9, 10, *16*
withdrawnness 18n6

Xu, Wenhao *117*, *131*

Yang Li *26*, *143*
Yingzhi, Caryn *215*, *222*, *223*
York, Megan *230*, *231*, *232*, *233*

Zabbaleen garbage collectors (Cairo) 149–150, 150n67, *151*, 164
Zamalek Island (Cairo) 141, 182, *see also* Casr El Nil Bridge
Zhang, Chi *159*, *165*
Zhang, Gu *165*
Zhang, Xinyue *173*
Zhang, Zehua *38*, *50*, *51*
Zhou, Jingyi *246*, *247*
Zhou, Yuanyi *56*, *65*, *75*, *76*, *77*, *78*
Zhu, Sihan *123*, *128*
Zmich, Molly *31*, *234*, *235*, *236*, *237*